これはダンスか？
Is this Dance?
「大野一雄」は終わらない
"Kazuo Ohno" is still among us.

1968年 ｜ 稽古場にて ｜ 撮影：ボブ藤崎
1968, Kazuo Ohno Dance Studio. photo: Bob Fujisaki

本書の編纂に多大なるご協力を賜った大野ファミリー、捜真女学校、上星川幼稚園、写真家、関係者の皆さんに心より感謝を捧げる。

We would like to express our heartfelt thanks to the Ohno family, the Soshin Girls' School, the Kamihoshikawa Kindergarden, as well as the various photographers and all those who helped to compile this book.

日常の奇跡

武田 文

若山美術館 館長

　本書は、昨年若山美術館で開催した『これはダンスか？「大野一雄」
は終わらない。大野一雄日常の糧展』をきっかけとして発見された新たな
資料と既存資料と併せて編纂したものである。

　『日常の糧』は、大野一雄の作品『ラ・アルヘンチーナ頌』の第二章の
タイトルより引用したものだ。敬虔なクリスチャンであった大野一雄にとって
「日常」とは存在し続けるもの、「糧」は存在を支えるもの。日常の中に舞踏
家の変容があるというのだ。大野一雄はありふれた身の回りに存在する日
常を大切にした。それはまるで小さな種が沢山の恩恵を受け枝葉を伸ばし、
葉を生い茂らす、当たり前の日常の出来事、それこそが奇跡であり、私達ひ
とりひとりのうえにも同じように存在する大切な生活である。その生きる姿こ
そ、踊ることそのものだったのであろう。そんな彼のプライベートの部分を前
面に取り上げ、大野一雄を知ってもらう試みとして同展は開催したのだった。
函館生まれで、お母さんが好きで、生徒に負けないくらい足が速い先生で、
ダンスを共にした女学校の先生で、いつも庭の草木の手入れをして、近所
の幼稚園でクリスマスのサンタクロースになって子供の内に居続けた…

　大野一雄はそんなありふれた日々の生活を、丁寧に生きることの大事さを
小さな種として、私達の足元にいつもある土の上にも蒔いてくれたにちがいない。

Everyday Miracles

Aya Takeda
Wakayama Art Museum Director

In addition to existing materials that were discovered for the *Is this Dance? Kazuo Ohno is still among us —The Kazuo Ohno exhibition "Daily Bread" : the life of the Butoh dancer who passed away at the age of 103* held at Wakayama Art Museum in 2018, this publication collates and compiles newly acquired materials.

The title *Daily Bread* is taken from the second segment of Kazuo Ohno's magnum opus *Admiring La Argentina*. As a lifelong devout Christian, Kazuo Ohno viewed "bread" as that which sustains our continued "daily" existence. In everyday life the Butoh dancer undergoes transformation. Kazuo Ohno deeply cherished everyday life in which our lives are anchored. Its branches extend and its leaves grow like a tiny plant receiving numerous benefits, and as with everyday events, they are all miracles. There is an equally precious life around each and every one of us. Kazuo Ohno's living figure was dance itself. The exhibition sought to highlight to Kazuo Ohno's private sphere and thereby make the public more aware the man behind the dancer. Born in Hakodate in Hokkaido, Kazuo Ohno was extremely close to his mother. As a teacher he was a faster runner than his students. He taught dance and danced together with his pupils at a girl's school in Yokohama, all while taking constant care of the plants in his garden and playing the role of Santa Claus among the children in his neighborhood kindergarden at Christmas.

Kazuo Ohno sew the idea of cherishing life and the everyday in the soil at our feet like small seeds.

目次 | CONTENTS

幼稚園
The Kindergarden ⋯⋯⋯⋯⋯⋯⋯ 008

稽古場
Keiko-ba [Rehearsal Studio] ⋯⋯⋯ 016

老人と海
The Old Man and the Sea ⋯⋯⋯ 024

イエスの招き
An Invitation to Jesus ⋯⋯⋯⋯ 042

100歳
Centenary Birthday ⋯⋯⋯⋯⋯ 058

衣装
Costumes ⋯⋯⋯⋯⋯⋯⋯⋯⋯ 064

アントニア・メルセ
Antonia Mercé, a.k.a. La Argentina ⋯⋯ 072

ボイラー室
Boiler Room ⋯⋯⋯⋯⋯⋯⋯⋯ 082

聖劇
The Nativity Play ⋯⋯⋯⋯⋯⋯ 090

ラ・アルヘンチーナ頌
Admiring La Argentina ⋯⋯⋯⋯ 098

体育教員
PE Teacher ⋯⋯⋯⋯⋯⋯⋯⋯⋯ 108

モダンダンス
Modern Dance ⋯⋯⋯⋯⋯⋯⋯ 114

戦争体験
Wartime Experience ⋯⋯⋯⋯⋯ 126

死海
The Dead Sea ⋯⋯⋯⋯⋯⋯⋯ 132

家族
Family ⋯⋯⋯⋯⋯⋯⋯⋯⋯⋯ 138

花、草、動物
Flowers, Plants,and Animals ⋯⋯⋯ 148

大野一雄からの手紙
Letters from Kazuo Ohno

ヘミングウェイへ
A letter to Ernest Hemingway ⋯⋯⋯ 030

ナンシーから
A letter from Nancy ⋯⋯⋯⋯⋯ 050

弟子・山口直永へ
A letter to his student,
Naoe Yamaguchi ⋯⋯⋯⋯⋯⋯ 123

戦線より
A Letter from the Warfront ⋯⋯⋯⋯ 130

大野一雄を語る
Interviews with those who knew Kazuo Ohno personally

インタビュー1 上星川幼稚園
（三戸部恵美子、岩村加恵子）
INTERVIEW 1 Kamihoshikawa
Kindergarden
(Emiko Mitobe, Kaeko Iwamura) ⋯⋯ 014

インタビュー2 天野 功
INTERVIEW 2 Isao Amano ⋯⋯⋯⋯ 056

インタビュー3 中島昭子
INTERVIEW 3 Akiko Nakajima ⋯⋯⋯ 080

インタビュー4 大野美加子
INTERVIEW 4 Mikako Ohno ⋯⋯⋯ 088

インタビュー5 大野悦子
INTERVIEW 5 Etsuko Ohno ⋯⋯⋯ 106

インタビュー6 ヨネヤマママコ
INTERVIEW 6 Mamako Yoneyama ⋯⋯ 146

1980年代｜稽古場にて
1980s, Kazuo Ohno Dance Studio

本書はアーカイヴ資料を網羅する意図はなく、また写真集を目指すものでもない。しかし、雑然としながら、どこまでも温かく、いまも確かな「大野一雄」の空気を伝えることができればと思っている。

This book is not intended as a showcase for archive materials nor as a photo collection. We do hope, however, to be able to convey Kazuo Ohno's truly diverse and charismatic presence, which persists to this very day.

幼稚園
The Kindergarden

横浜市保土ヶ谷の自宅に近い上星川幼稚園の
クリスマス会で、園児達のもとをサンタクロース
になって訪れた。1960年代から毎年続けた。親
子二代で見た人もいる。

Kazuo Ohno visited the children at the
Kamihoshikawa Kindergarden near his
home in Hodogaya in Yokohama to play
Santa Claus in the annual Christmas Play. He
continued this tradition on an annual basis
since the 1960s. Some children of former
students also had occasion to see him perform Santa Claus.

001

002

001-002.　1960年代｜上星川幼稚園の講堂にて
1960s, Kamihoshikawa Kindergarden's chapel.

09

003

004

005

003-004.　1998年｜お面の顔が怖くて泣き出す子もいた｜
　　　　　撮影：竹内北子
　　　　　1998, Children frightened by Santa Claus's mask. photo: Kitako Takeuchi

005.　幼稚園のチャペルの前で
　　　Christmas Tree in front of Kindergarden chapel.

006

007

007. 1989年 | クリスマス礼拝で踊る | 撮影：ペーター・ゼンペル
1989, Dancing at the Christmas Pageant. photo: Peter Sempel

008

009

008-009. 1989年｜妻チエと｜撮影：ペーター・ゼンペル
1989, with his wife Chie. photo: Peter Sempel

010

011

010. 2000年｜園児たちとお別れの挨拶
2000, Santa bidding the Kindergarden children goodbye.

011. 2006年まで続けた
Kazuo Ohno continued this tradition until 2006.

インタビュー1

上星川幼稚園
（三戸部恵美子、岩村加恵子）

三戸部：クリスマスの前に打ち合わせに行くんですね。大野先生のご自宅に。12月の始めにクリスマスがあって、11月23日の勤労感謝の日の前のときに、必ずおうちに行くと、奥様がいらして。
岩村：ココアね。
三：ココア。ココアっていうか、紅茶、ミルクティ。そうでしたでしょ。
岩：お砂糖、いっぱいいれてくださって。
三：お砂糖をいっぱい。そして打ち合わせをするんですけれども、その打ちあわせのときに、(私達が)こうしてください、ああしてくださいって言うの。私達はこの曲で、何曲です、よろしくお願いしますって言うと、マヘリア・ジャクソン、ね。まずクリスマスをやるには、この曲を聴いてください、から始まるんです。レコードをかけて、マヘリア・ジャクソンのオー・ホーリー・ナイト。先生も自然とこう、踊り出して。大野先生の世界にも、入っちゃうんですよ。お膳。お膳というか、お母さんの、あの世界のお話が始まるんです。すべてこのお膳の中に、私はいるって言って。お膳の上に乗って、お母さんっていう、ね？　毎回、そのお話を聞きました。そして、愛なんだって言って、この中に、悲しいとき、嬉しいとき、結婚式のお膳。なんか、本にも書いてありましたよね？　お膳。ご葬儀のときもお膳って。私はこのお膳の中に、そしてそのお膳に私は乗るんですよって。先生、お膳の上なんか乗っちゃうんですか、なんてね、みんな若い先生たちが、えっお膳の上に乗っちゃうの、なんて言うと。愛がすべてここの中に入ってるっていうお話で、クリスマスのこうしましょうああしましょうっていうのは、ほとんどなかったんです、お話は。
三：それから町内の運動会。町内の運動会、お祭り？
岩：仮装行列、地元の子供、うちの近くの子供達と仮装行列して。

三：衣装つけてね。
岩：歩き方をね。グラウンドの、町内の運動会のグラウンドの周り方を、歩き方を大野先生教えてくださって、みんなそれに付いて、お魚だのね、なんだのって。

三：大野先生がいらして、上星川は良くなったって言った方がいらっしゃるのね。大野先生って、本当に、草むしりをしてたり。通られた方にお話かけてたんだと思うんですね。町内の人が、この地域に素晴らしい、人間的に、素晴らしい人がいるっていって。大野先生のことなんか、何にも知らない方ですよ、踊りやってるとか。どこで会ったんですかと言ったら、その坂のところにね、まだ、そんなにお年じゃないころよね。
岩：いらした間もなくかな。近所では評判でしたよ、大野先生のご家族は。親切で。猫の世話もあるし。それからすごく…
三：あたたかいのね。あのお孫さんにしろ。
岩：先生の家族はね、もう本当に、皆さん。
三：で、町内の人がみんな大好きだったです。知らない方々がね。
岩：そうねえ。そして後で有名な方だっていうので、びっくりなさって。
三：大野先生が寝込まれてから、ね、行って。
岩：讃美歌を一緒に歌ったわね。先生が、ご家族いらっしゃらないときとかに行くと、讃美歌を一緒に歌って、そうすると、気づいているかどうかはわからないけど、一緒に声だけはね、先生、出してくださって。
三：あーって声出してくださった。

2016.4.25

三戸部恵美子、岩村加恵子｜上星川幼稚園を経営。大野一雄の教え子。姉妹で一雄にソシアルダンスを習ったこともある。

INTERVIEW 1

Kamihoshikawa Kindergarden

(Emiko Mitobe, Kaeko Iwamura)

Mitobe: We always used to visit Sensei's home to discuss the Christmas pageant the day before Labour Thanksgiving Day. His wife invariably offered us...

Iwamura: Cocoa.

M: Cocoa or milk tea, wasn't it?

I: With lots of sugar.

M: Yes, with lots of sugar. During our discussion we would make several requests about the music to use. Sensei would then propose Mahalia Jackson and asked us to listen to her music for the preparation. After he put on Jackson's *O Holy Night*, he started to dance. He was spirited away. And he would talk about the *Ozen* [a small eating table] and about his mother. He always spoke of how his entire existence was linked to the Ozen and of coming in contact with his mother whenever he knelt on top of the table. He spoke of how it symbolized everything: love, joy, sadness, and marriage. He wrote about how the Ozen was linked to life and death. The younger teachers were taken aback to hear that he would sit on the Ozen during a performance and asked whether it was true. And he spoke about how the Ozen was filled with love. He rarely mentioned the Christmas pageant.

M: There was the local athletic meeting.

I: It included a fancy dress parade. He would instruct the local children for it.

M: He would have them put on costumes.

I: He taught the children how to walk in a procession in the local sports grounds. The children, some in fish costumes, would follow him around the grounds.

M: A neighbour mentioned that Kamihoshikawa had improved thanks to Ohno-sensei. He would weed the garden and greet those walking by his house. The neighbours mentioned how a wonderful person had moved into the area without knowing anything about Ohno-sensei's dance. On a human level, they found him wonderful. On asking where this person was living, they replied up the hill. He wasn't that old at the time, was he?

I: It was soon after he moved in. They spoke of him as a kind elderly gentleman. The Ohno household had a good reputation for their kindness and for taking care of cats.

M: And his grandchildren were so warm-hearted.

I: Sensei's entire family are truly so warm-hearted.

M: His neighbours were fond of him, even those who didn't know about him.

I: Yes, they were. And whenever they learnt at just how famous he was, they were astounded.

M: We visited him after he became bedbound.

I: When his family was absent, we would sing hymns together. We were unsure of whether he recognized us, and yet he joined us in song.

M: Yes, he sang along with us.

April 25, 2016

Emiko Mitobe, Kaeko Iwamura Directors of the Kamihoshikawa Kindergarden and former students of Kazuo Ohno under whom they both trained for social dance.

稽古場
Keiko-ba [Rehearsal Studio]

勤めていた学校でいらなくなった窓枠と廃材を使って自宅の隣に建てた。壁と家具は白ペンキで自分で塗った。ペンキ塗りは得意だった。

Ohno built his rehearsal studio in the back garden of his home using window frames and demolition material from the school where he was employed. Given he was a good painter, Ohno painted the walls and furniture with white paint.

013.

013. 1961年｜建設中の稽古場
1961, Rehearsal studio under construction.

014

015

014. 『わたしのお母さん』1981年初演に向けての稽古、中央に土方巽、手前に大野慶人
1981, Rehearsal before premiere of *My Mother*. Tatsumi Hijikata is seated to the right of Ohno, Yoshito Ohno is in the foreground.

015. 1980年｜間口3間半、奥行き7間半の板張りの白い空間｜撮影：神山貞次郎
1980, the white-walled rehearsal space.
photo : Teijiro Kamiyama

016. 1980年｜研究生の稽古｜撮影：神山貞次郎
    1980, In rehearsal at his studio.
    photo : Teijiro Kamiyama

017. 1985年｜『ラ・アルヘンチーナ頌』稽古、中央にバンドネオン演奏 池田光夫｜撮影：ヌリート・マッソン＝セキネ
    1985, rehearsing *Admiring La Argentina*. The bandoneon player Mitsuo Ikeda is seated in the middle. photo: Nourit Masson-Sékiné

018.

018. 80年代の稽古場｜椅子の上にあぐらをかく、得意のポーズ｜写真：ヌリート・マッソン＝セキネ
1980s rehearsal studio, Ohno posing in his chair. photo: Nourit Masson-Sékiné

019.

020.

019-020. 1980年｜最初に大野一雄が話をして、音をかけて研究生が踊る｜撮影：神山貞次郎
1980, Ohno first talks to students, then plays music for them to dance. photo: Teijiro Kamiyama

021

022

021. 1980年代｜海外から多くの研究生を迎えた
 1980s, Many overseas students study with Ohno.

022. 1980年代｜衣装や小道具が雑然と置かれている
 1980s, All sorts of stage props and costumes in the studio.

023

024

023. 1980年代
1980s, Ohno rehearsing at the studio.

024. 稽古場の棚
Shelves in the rehearsal studio.

23

老人と海
The Old Man and the Sea

1959年の群舞作品。長男幸人はマグロ役、次男慶人が少年役でデビューした。ヘミングウェイに手紙を書いて、写真と共に送った。本人に届いたろうか。

A group dance work performed in 1959. The eldest son Yukito made his stage debut in the role of a tuna, and the second son Yoshito played the role of the young boy. Ohno wrote a letter to Hemingway and sent it along with some photos. Did he ever receive it?

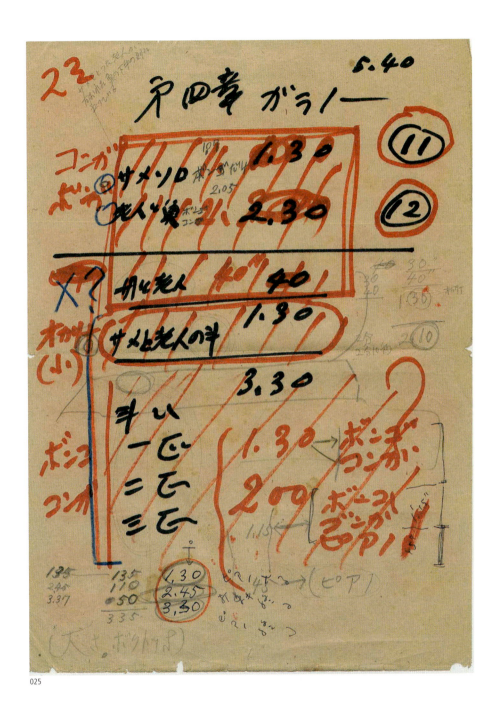

025-029. 『老人と海』創作ノート｜作品の構成や動きのヒントが書かれている
Working notes for *The Old Man and the Sea* with ideas for movements and structure.

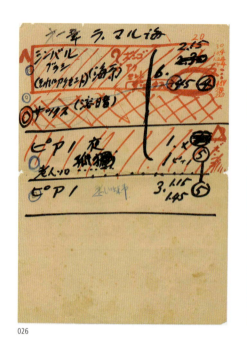
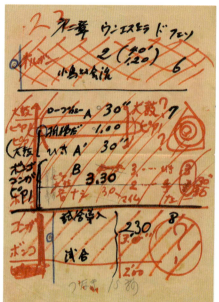

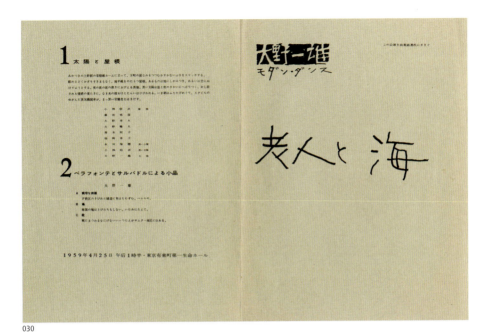

030. 大野一雄モダンダンス公演プログラム
Program for Kazuo Ohno's Modern Dance Performance.

031. サン写真新聞の公演評｜1959年4月30日
Critique in *San* Photo Magazine, 30 April 1959.

032

033

034

035

032.-033. 大野慶人 Yoshito Ohno	034. 1959年｜マグロ役の長男幸人(手前)と少年役の次男慶人(奥) 1959, His eldest son Yukito in the foreground in the role of the tuna and Yoshito in the role of the young boy.	035. 1959年｜老人役の大野一雄と船を踊る3人の女性 Ohno in the role of the Old Man with 3 female dancers in the role of the skiff.

036.

036. 1959年4月25日｜東京・日比谷の第一生命ホールにて、1回かぎりの公演だった
The one-off performance took place on 25 April 1959 at the Daichi Seimei Hall in Hibiya, Tokyo.

大野一雄からの手紙

ヘミングウェイへ

1

敬愛するヘミングウエー様

私は先生の著書の愛讀者であり特に老人と海に記された

力強く愛情があり　そして孤獨でありながら孤獨でないあの老人

に言葉では言いつくせない魅力を感じあの老人の幸を祈るものです

私の家が祖父や父の時代に三本マストの帆船を仕立てゝ遠く

まで出かけ漁業に從事していたためでもありますが魚釣りに非常に

興味を持つております。

永遠の敗北を表徴する旗印としかみえなかつたつきはぎたらけの帆

不漁續きであつても老人にとつて（毎日が新しい日）であつたとゆう事

いたましい事ではあるが最後まで鮫と斗つたあのフアイト、すべても

轉んでも又立上がつた老人の精神力がどこから生れるのでしようか

私は舞踊を通じて老人と海に自分を投入することによつて私の肉体で

私の魂で直接にそれを感得したいと思いました。申おくれましたが

私は日本の一個の貧しいモダンダンサーです。第二次大戦后四回自分の

リサイタルを開いて参りました。現在私はバプテスト派の女子高校に勤務

舞踊を生徒に教えております。私は私の愛している私の学校の生徒達に

老人と海とその心を傳へるために先生の著書、文献をよみ私で出来

るだけの研究をしました　老人と海に感動し共に先生の著書について

研究して来た友人があります　池宮信夫君といゝます　彼は平凡社

とゆ（原文ママ）出版社で百科事典を編集している青年で舞踊演劇テレビ等で

台本と評論の筆をとつております　彼と私は老人と海からの感

動について毎晩語り合ひました　私は舞踊家として老人と海に

全くとりつかれてしまつたのです　到底舞踊で表現することは不可能な

事だと始めはあきらめつゝ仕事が手につきませんでした　しかし

老人の乗つているボートを三人の女性によつて表現することにより

舞踊化の可能性を見出しました　私はラ．マルについて(p.32-p.33)書かれている箇所

特に（それは海みづからどうしようもないことぢやないか　月が海を支配しているんだ

それが人間の女たちを支配する様に）をよんでいる時

ボートを三人の女性によつて表現することを思いつきました

昨年始め基本的動きのかたまりをいくつかまとめようやう

舞踊他の構想をまとめるに到りましたので

敬愛する ヘミングウェー 様へ

私は先生の著書の愛読者であり特に老人と海に記された
力強く愛情がありそして孤独でありながら孤独でないあの老人
に言葉では言いつくせない魅力を感じあの老人の事を祈るものです
私の家が祖父や父の時代に三本マストの帆船を仕立て、遠く
まで出かけ漁業に従事していたためでもありますが奥釣りに格別た
興味を持っております

暗永の敗北を象徴する錨印としかつ又まがった
不漁続きであっても老人にとって毎日が新しい日であったとゆう事
いたましい事ではあるが最後まで鮫と斗ったあの ファイト、すべっても
待人も又立上った老人の精神力がどこから来るのでしょうか
私は舞踊を通じて老人と海に自分を投入することによって私の肉体で
私の恋で直接にそれを感得したいと思いました 申おくれましたが
私は日本の一個り貧しいモダンダンサーです。第二次大戦后四回目の
リサイタルを開いて参りました。地在私はバプテスト派の女子高校に勤務
勤務で生徒に教しております。私は私の愛している私の学校の生徒達に
老人と海とその心を伝える為に之迄の著書、文献...
...だけの研究をしました 老人と海に感動したに先生の著書について
研究した先生友人があります 池宮信夫君といます 彼は平凡社
と云お版社で百科事典を編集している群で...演劇、テレビ等で
台本と評論の筆をとっております 彼と私は老人と海からの感
動力について毎晩話合へました 私は舞踊家として老人と海に
全くとりつかれてしまったのです 地在、舞踊で表現することは不可能な
事だと始めはあきらめつつ、仕事が手につきませんでした しかし
老人の変っている ボートを三人の女性によって表現することにより
...

ボートを三人の女性によって表現することを思いつきました
昨年始め墓象が初きの かたまり をいくつか まとめ よろやう
舞踊他の構想をまとめる に到りましたので

037

037.-041.　ヘミングウェイへの手紙原稿｜作品の台本を担当した池宮信夫が保管していた
Ohno's original letter to Hemingway which was kept by Nobuo Ikemiya, script writer.

2

池宮君に依頼し音楽照明の細部に亘る台本を脚色してもらいました
私は1953年以来舞踊の作品と表現技術の関係について大変なやみ
ながら研究して参りましたが　老人と海を讀み多大のサゼッションを得
ました。作品については骨格より御知らせする事が出来ませんが若し
先生にサゼッションを與へて頂けたら私は幸この上もありません
私の部屋には先生御夫妻の寫眞と映画老人と海の切抜きを
かざつて私の励ましとしております。
さて私は(昨年)台本が完成する前後から作品全体の振付にとりかゝりました
作品をつくる上に於て私の最も苦しんだのは老人であります　老人の
一歩一歩の歩みに老人の生きている世界がにぢんでいなければいきいきと
しないとゆう事でした。私は寫眞で御覧の様にほつそりとしております。しかし
私はダンサーとしてのパーソナリテイを必死の思ひで此の老人に賭けております
いまさら変へようのない貧弱な体躯のサイズが観客の目に全く感じられないような
舞台空間を必ず創造したいと思いますが　このことは老人を理解すること
老人の生きている世界を理解することによつて必ず実現したいと決心して
おります。老人の表現と共にこれ以上に苦しんだのはボートの表現でした
一見に舟とわかる構成を基本とし無生物としての表現の制約の上にたつて
老人の刻々に変化する立場と心配を如何に表現するかとゆうことに苦しんでいますが
(ボートが無生物であるとゆう制約を超えて老人との結び
つきに面白さがあります面白さとゆうより切実な人生があると思います)
老人の舟出に於ける舟への無意識の信頼と海に出る老人のよろこび
最初のひき等いたる所克服しなけばならない舟の表現上の困難な
問題が次々とありますが眞実こそこれらの困難を解決する鍵だと
考へ逐次構成を進めております
弧獨を感じた時　あの子がいたらなあとゆうくだりに　二匹のまぐろ(まかじき)との
悲しい出来事を結びつけました。舞台の前で老人は垂直に糸をたれ
後方では花輪のやうな(天井からたれさがつた)えさのオブジエに雌のまぐろがひつかゝる所は
p60「この出来事は俺の出会つた一番悲しい事件だ」俺たちは雌にあやまつて直ぐばらしてしまつたが
とゆう感銘をもつて振付し演出されております

◎手紙とは別　海にある限り最良の時。其の海との結びつきは
老人にとつては絶対のものであつた自分の思ふまゝになる時があつたとしても
最愛の手にゆられるボートに載つた老人は丁度ゆりかごの様な
関係でないか?　ゆりかごを通して感ずる海

2

池宮君に依頼し音楽照明の細部に亘る台本を脚色してもらいました
私は1953年以来 舞踊の作品と表現技術の関係について大変ながみ
ながら研究して参りましたが 老人と海を読み 多大のサゼッションを得
ました。作品については 骨格より御知らせする事が出来ませんが若し
先生にサゼッションを与えて頂けたら私は幸 この上もありません
私の部屋には先笔場夫妻の墨蹟と映画 老人と海の切抜等を
かざって私の励みとしております。
さて私は 此事が完成する前から 作品全体の振付にかかりました
作品をつくる上に於て私の最も苦しんだのは老人であります 老人の
一挙一動の歩みに老人の生きている世界がにちんでいなければいけないと
しないとより事でした。私は高杰で御覧の様に ほっそりとしております。しかし
私はダンサーとしてのパーソナリティを 此死の思いでした老人に賭けております
いまさら憂いようがない 食籠石体躯のサイズが観客の目に全く感じられないような
舞台空間を必ず創造したいと思いますが そのことは老人を理解すること
老人の生きている世界を理解することになって必ず実現したいと決心して
おります。老人が漁獲と共にこれ以上に苦しんだのは ボートが完璧で全
一見して母とわかる構成を基本とし 無生路 としての表現の制約の上にたって
老人の刻々に変化する立場と心理を如何に実現するかという事に苦しんでいますが
老人の母親に対する 母への 無意識の信頼と海に出る老人とのよろこび
最初の 付手 いたる所 克服しなければならない母の表現上の困難な
内容が次々と出ますが 確実ここ これらの困難を解決する気持と
老い進次 構成を進めております
孤独と感じた時 ありそうがたいなるという くなりに… 二匹のまぐろとの
悲しい出来事を結びつけました。舞台の若い老人は 重連ん糸を元れ
では花壇のや 考えのオブジェん 母のまぐろがりつかける所 は
「この出来事は 俺の 生きった 最悲しい事件だ」俺んように 俺にお帰って
という感銘をもって振付し 演出されております

3

老人が死斗することによつて頭がもうろう(p111 意識があやしくなる)として来た時に老人が大魚と
会話する場面に始めて大魚が舞台に登場いたしますが此の大魚の役は
私の長男(シヤンソン及ラテン物の歌手)が受け持ち
(老人の愛してる)少年は私の次男が受持ちます。
サメは男性ダンサーで單数ですが照明及三人の女性の表現にたすけられ
複数のイメージとして象徴的に表現します
腕角力(ズモウ)に出て来るニグロは永い間私と共に舞踊を研究している
大学の(舞踊の)プロフエツサーが担当します。
私は極めて理解の足りず又力のたりない者ですがクリスチヤンとしての
信仰と舞踊に対する信念により(其上先生の画えた最も好ましい生き方をした老人に励まされつゝ)
私の最善をつくし眞実と感銘を
築いて行き度いと思つております。私はあの老人が
セットは老人の小屋だけ　小道具は雌かぢきを釣りあげるために
用ひるヒゲをかくした美しい鰯のえさ　とラストシーンに用ひる大魚の
骸骨の二つだけです。
舞台照明の転換操作によつて夜明け海辺海中など暗示します
音楽は池宮君のプランにより　ボンゴ　コンガ　シンバル　ピアノ
サツクス　オカリナにとどめ　作曲者安田収吾(シユウゴ)君のアイデイアにより
特殊な音色の出るオルガンの効果を老人と小鳥との会話の時に限り
ピアノとの二重奏に使用いたします　オカリナは私が吹奏しボンゴは
主として少年の老人に對する愛情と友情を表現するもので少年を演ずる
私の次男が演奏致します。録音は(私の友人である専門の技術家によつて)昨年十月に終り今は
音楽を
テープにより演奏しつゝ　けいこを續けております。
(これらのスタツフはいづれも私の親しい友人で懸命に老人と海を研究し最善の状態によつて公
演されることを心掛けております)
本年4月25日(土)午后2時東京の中心にある第一生命ホール
(定員600)にて公演を予定しております。
先生此の手紙が大変おくれた失禮をおわび申上げます
昨年秋に公演致したく思い懸命に努力致しました　資金の調達とゆう
問題もありましたが遂に作品が出来上るまでに到りませんでした
今は全く新たな気持と勇気をもつて作品に取り組み最近やうやく
見透しを得るに至りました　先生の立派な作品から受けた感銘
ではありますが私の力と努力がたりないために先生の名誉が

039

040

4

傷つけられる様な事があつてはと思ひ今少し可能性をみ出してから
今少し良くなつてからと思いつゝ今日に至りました
老人と海に感銘し心から協力して下さるスタツフ　キヤスト一同と共に
アンサンブルを築きあげることによつて此等の困難を必ず克服致します
資金が許せばせめて数日連續して公演を持ち日本のヘミングウエー
フアン及在日外人の方にも見て頂き度いのですが思ふにまかせず一回
だけのリサイタルより開けません事を深くお詫び申上げます　私は
今回のリサイタルだけで公演を終らず長い時間をかけて此の作品を
更らに更らに将来良い作品に仕上げ度いと思つております。
今回の公演に先生をお招き出来たら　どんなにか素晴しい事だろうと
空想するだけでも胸がはずみます　萬一チヤンスがございましたら
日本へお出掛け下さいませんか　私は極めて貧しい者ですが家族
一同此の公演に協力して下さる一同と共に心一ぱいの歡迎を申上げたいと思います
私も公演までに出来るだけの資金ぐりをして8ミリか16ミリ
のフイルムに収め音楽のテープと共にお送り致し度いと考へております
上演のお許しを心からお願ひ申上げます
最後に先生御夫妻の御健康と御活躍をはるかにお祈りし
私のつたない公演になにとぞ寛大なはげましを頂けます様にお願いいたす次第でございます。

5

参考までに 構成のあらましを つぎに記します

プロローグ
　　貧しい小屋で寝ている老人
84日も魚が一匹もとれず　永遠の敗北感と絶望的な種｜とがしみ込んでいたあったがうすれすぎた'517
しかし　老人にとって毎日毎日は全く新しい日であった
　　別名

才一景　ラ・マル
　　　　ラ・マル（海）
　　　　最初のひき
　　　　星の住居のうすと奥は夜中連絡を喜びかった　P56-3
　　　　悲しい事件

才二景　ウン エスペランドフエソ（星の判決）
　　　　小鳥との会話
　　　　やられた引き付けられた老人　やくざな魚
　　　　ローフーリエー
　　　　ニグロとの思い　苦しみながら　無意識に牛をかす老人

才三景　ジュエゴ（試合）
　　　　右の掌が…もえる持ル病に、ついに奥は学をつくてる
　　　　死斗　奥とのコミックな会話
　　　　血まみれな斗…　俺たちがいやなら詩んだがかった

才四景　ガラノーだ（鮫台）
　　　　サメ ソロ　老人と大魚とのデュエット
　　　　サメと老人のデュエット　鮫との斗…
　　　　井のましみ．最後まで戦う老人

エピローグ　また小屋と少年　賢者というべ老人をみに注するや少年
　　　　老人は少年をみない　少年も老人をみない
　　　　かいこうを捨てお屋へ帰る老人　立ろつくす少年

5

御参考までに構成のあらましをつぎに記します

プロローグ
貧しい小屋で寝ている老人
84日も魚が一匹もつれず
P2 永遠の敗北を象徴する旗印としかみえなかつたあのつぎはぎだらけの帆の様な老人
しかし老人にとて(原文ママ)毎日毎日は全く新しい日であつた
船出

第一景　　ラ．マル
p32　　　ラ．マル(海)
p49　　　最初のひき
p56-3　　星の位置からすると魚は夜中進路を変えなかつた P56-3
p60　　　悲しい事件

第二景　　　　p87 ウン エスプエラドフエソ(骨の刺戟)
p67-68　小鳥との会話
p69　　　やにわにひき倒された老人　　　p73 やくざな手
　　　　　ロープウエー
p89-2　ニグロとの思出　　　p83 苦しみながら　無意識に手をかざす老人

第三景　p87 ジュエゴ(試合)
p107　　右の掌が　　もえる様に痛い　p79 ついに魚は姿をみせる
　　　　死斗　　魚とのコミツクな会話
　　　　血まみれな斗い　　俺はたしかにやつの心臓にさわつた

第四景　p142 ガラノーだ(鮫だ)
　　　　　サメのソロ　老人と大魚のデユエツト
　　　　　サメと老人のデユエツト　鮫との斗い
　　　　　舟の悲しみ　最後まで戦う老人

エピローグ　ボロ小屋と少年　骸骨をひつぱる老人をみて泣きだす少年
　　　　　　老人は少年をみない　少年も老人をみない
　　　　　　がいこつを捨てゝ小屋へ帰る老人　立ちつくす少年

Letters from Kazuo Ohno
A letter to Ernest Hemingway

Dear Mr Hemingway,

I am a great admirer of your work, notably *The Old Man and the Sea*.

That old man, whose charm cannot be expressed through words, is deeply passionate and solitary, and yet not solitary. I pray for the happiness of that old man.

I have a deep interest in fishing, given that my ancestors, back in the days of my grandfather and father, were involved in the fishing industry and built a three-masted fishing vessel and went way offshore to fish.

The sail looks like the flag that symbolizes permanent defeat.

Irrespective of whether the old man doesn't make a catch, ("every day is a new day"), it's frustrating, but how impressive that he ultimately fought it out with the sharks.

Whether he slips or rises again, where does the old man derive his mental vigour for that fight?

Through dance I immersed myself into *The Old Man and the Sea* and wanted to feel it directly in my soul. I apologise for not introducing myself, but I am just a down-in-the heels modern dancer in Japan. Since the end of World War II, I have given four dance recitals. I am currently working for a Baptist girls' school where I teach dance to students. In order to inject the spirit of *The Old Man and the Sea* into my beloved students, I have read your books and writings and studied them whenever I can. A friend of mine has studied your works and is equally moved by *The Old Man and the Sea*. His name is Nobuo Ikemiya. He works as an editor at a publishing company called Heibonsha where he is collating an encyclopaedia. He is a young man who writes reviews of dance, theatre and television, and

has written scenarios and criticism. Every evening, he and I discuss the passion emanating from *The Old Man and the Sea*. As a dancer, I was utterly hooked on *The Old Man and the Sea*; I felt I couldn't possibly express it through dance and was soon to give up, unable to focus on the task at hand. But, by using three women to express the skiff in which the old man fishes, I discovered the possibility of staging it through dance. The idea of expressing the skiff by using three human women occurred to me particularly after reading the *La Mar* section pp. 32-33 ("if she did wild or wicked things it was because she could not help them, the moon affects the sea just in the same way as it affects a woman").

Given such, I was thinking to finalize some basic movements at the beginning of last year, for I had already settled on the concept for the dance and other related matters.

I commissioned Ikemiya-san to write a stage adaptation with details for the musical accompaniment and stage lighting. Though I've faced challenges in how to interlink dance works and expressive techniques ever since 1953, I have pursued this research and I was deeply inspired on reading *The Old Man and the Sea*. I can only inform you about the adaptation's basic structure, so I couldn't be happier if you might kindly provide me with some suggestions. A photo of you and your wife, as well as a newspaper clipping about the film *The Old Man and the Sea*, adorn my room and act as an encouragement for me.

Recently (last year) I became involved in choreographing the entire piece, around the time the adaptation had been completed. The old man's character, the universe he inhabited caused the most difficulty in creating the piece, for I had to make his each and every step vibrant. As you can see in the photograph, I am slender. And yet, my personality as a dancer is wagering desperately on this old man. While I truly want to create a stage space in which the audience cannot discern my body's miserable size, which in any case cannot be changed now, I am determined to have them grasp the old man, and to understand the world in which he lives. Aside from the old man, I had greater difficulties expressing the skiff. Using a structure in which the skiff can be understood at first glance, and yet restrict its expression as an inanimate object, I struggle with how to express the old man's constantly changing behaviour and worries. (I think that if the skiff goes beyond its limitations as an inanimate object, how it links with the old man will be interesting, or more precisely what we will have is a poignant human being.)

Problems arose one after the other on being confronted with how to express the scene where he makes his first catch, or the old man's joy at being at sea, or his unconscious trust in the skiff, but truth is the key to solving such difficulties and I am proceeding to work on the piece with this belief in mind.

I linked the scene where the old man was feeling alone, and yearned for the presence of that young boy and the sad event involving the two tuna (marlins). At the front of the stage, the old man is threading the fishing line vertically while at the back (of the stage), a female tuna circles the gar-land-like baited object (hanging from the ceiling).

p. 60 "That was the saddest thing I ever saw." The boy too was sad; we begged her pardon and promptly butchered her. Deeply moved [by this scene] I will choreograph and perform it.

◎Aside from this letter, it is the best time as long as you are at sea. For the old man, the relationship with that sea was something absolute, even if at times he did get his own way, the old man on the skiff is swayed just like a cradle by his beloved hand, experiencing the sea through the cradle.

As the old man engaged in a mortal combat, his mind was becoming dimmer (his consciousness fading), the old man initiated a conversation with the large fish, the large fish will first appear onstage. My eldest son will play the role of this large fish (he is a singer of chanson and Latin music).
The young boy (the one the old man loves) will be played by my second son.
The role of the sharks will be played by a male dancer, assisted by the stage lighting and the three females' expressions that combined will symbolically express multiple images.
A professor of dance at a university, who has been studying under me, will take on the role of the negro who appears in the scene with the udezumou (wrist fight).

Although I'm extremely lacking in understanding or in power, my belief as a Christian in faith and in dance (inspired by the old man's most favourable lifestyle as depicted by you) makes me long to create a

39

profound and truthful impression and I will do my utmost.

In terms of a set for that old man, I will only have that old man's shack.
As for props, I will only use two, a beautiful sardine bait to catch the marlin, and a skeleton of the big fish in the final scene.
With the stage lighting, I will be able to hint at the sea, the seashore, and dawn, by regulating the [lighting] rig,
Staying with Ikemiya-san's concept, musical accompaniment will be provided by bongos, conga, cymbals, piano, saxophone, and ocarina. The composer Shugo Yasuda's idea is to confine an organ effect with a special tonal colour for the conversation between the old man and the small bird. We will use a piano for the duets. I myself will play the ocarina. Performed by the boy, the bongos will mostly be used to express the young boy's love and friendship for the old man, as interpreted by my second son. Recording was completed in October of last year (by my friend who is a technical specialist) and we are now using a taped version for rehearsals.
(The entire staff are on friendly terms with me and they will intensely study *The Old Man and the Sea* in order to ensure the best conditions for the performance.)

The performance is scheduled for 25 April (Saturday), 2:00 pm, at the Daiichi Seimei Hall in downtown Tokyo.
(Audience capacity: 600 people).
I do apologize for the tardiness of this letter to you.

I did my utmost to give a performance last fall.

Given I encountered a problem with borrowing the money, I was unable to stage the work in the end. Now I'm finally in a position to rework the piece with a completely fresh feeling and emboldened.
While deeply moved by your outstanding work, I am concerned that your honour will be sullied due to my lack of power and effort.

Though I mentioned the possibility that you might be offended, I do believe that we have now reached a stage where the work has somewhat improved. Jointly with my cast and staff, who are deeply impressed with *The Old Man and the Sea* and who will fully cooperate by building an ensemble, we will surely overcome those difficulties.
If funding allowed, I hoped to perform a run for at least a few days in Japan and have both Hemingway fans as well as foreigners resident in Japan come and see the performance. I deeply apologize for not being able to produce more than just one recital. I will use this recital as a springboard with which to improve this piece, and over time to continue working on it. My wish is to complete a good piece. What a wonderful thing it would be were I able to invite you to this performance; the very fact of thinking about it makes my heart bounce.

Should you have the opportunity, would you like to travel to Japan? Though my household is very poor, we would all extend you a heartfelt welcome and do everything in our power to produce the performance.
I'm going to gather as much money as possible before the performance, and would like to send you the 8mm or 16mm footage along with the recorded music on tape. I

sincerely ask for your permission to perform the piece.

Finally, I pray for you and your wife health and success.

It is my hope that you will be indulgent toward my poor-quality performance.

Below is a summary of the structure, for your reference.

Prologue

Old man sleeping in his rundown shack
Up to the 84 days without catching a fish.
p. 2 The old man who is like a patched-up sail that looked like the flag of permanent defeat
The old man....
And yet, each day for the old man was a completely new day.
Heading out to sea.

Part I *La Mar*

p. 32 *La Mar* (the sea)
p. 49 First tug on the line
p. 56-3 [Seen] from the stars, the fish did not change course overnight P. 56-3
P. 60 Sad event

Part II *Un Espuela de hueso* [bone spur] (p. 87) (impetus of the bones)
p. 67-68 Conversing with a small bird
p. 69 Suddenly the old man pulled down into the bow p. 73 Bloodied hand
Ropeway
p. 89-2 Thinking about the negro p. 83. The old man holding his hand unconsciously aloft

Part III *Juegos* (baseball games) (p. 87)
p. 107 Burning pain through his right palm
p. 79 The fish finally appears

Mortal combat— Communicative conversation with the tuna
A bloody battle   I surely stoked his heart

Part IV *Galano !* (Sharks!) (p. 142)
Shark solo, duet between the old man and the big fish
Shark and old man's duet. Combat with shark.
The miserable skiff, the old man who fought it out.

Epilogue

Rundown shack and the boy. The boy starts crying on seeing the old man with the skeleton.
The old man doesn't look at the boy; the boy doesn't look at the old man.
After abandoning the skeleton, the old man returns to his shack. The boy stands stock-still.

41

イエスの招き
An Invitation to Jesus

クリスチャンであり、ミッションスクールの教員だった。舞踏家として、ヨーロッパで公演をするときには、教会で踊りたいと願っていた。

Not only was Ohno a Christian, he also taught at a Baptist mission school. As a Butoh dancer, he yearned to perform in a church when on tour in Europe.

042. 1980年｜ナンシー・サン＝フィアクル教会｜撮影：神山貞次郎
1980, in Nancy Saint-Fiacre Church. photo: Teijiro Kamiyama

043.

043. 信仰と舞踏はひとつものである、と証を立てた｜撮影：神山貞次郎
Ohno testified that Butoh and faith are one and the same.　photo: Teijiro Kamiyama

044.
044. サン゠フィアクル教会の盲目のオルガニストとともに ｜ 撮影：神山貞次郎
With the blind organist at Saint-Fiacre Church. photo: Teijiro Kamiyama

045.
045. 教会内は信者でいっぱいだった｜撮影：神山貞次郎
The church was filled with the faithful. photo: Teijiro Kamiyama

046

047

048

046.-048.　写真：神山貞次郎
Dancing in Saint-Fiacre Church. photo: Teijiro Kamiyama

049

049. 1980年｜ナンシー国際演劇祭プログラム
Program for the 1980 Festival de Nancy.

1977年、ナンシーに行く前、土方巽の演出によって、大野一雄の身体の隅から隅まで、心の流れは駆け巡り、沈下し上昇し、炸裂して、目を見張るようなダンスとして繰り広げられるようになっていた。「ラ・アルヘンティーナ頌」が十全な姿となっていたのだ。

小倉正史（美術評論家）

In 1977, before travelling to Nancy, under the direction of Tatsumi Hijikata, *Admiring La Argentina* became the perfect guise for Kazuo Ohno's dance to thoroughly embody an explosive range of emotions.

Masashi Ogura, Art Critic

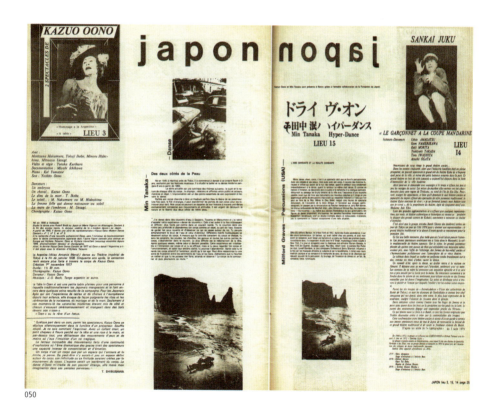

050.

050. 日本プログラムのひとつとして招聘された
Ohno was invited as part of the festival's Japanese program.

大野一雄からの手紙

ナンシーから

ナンシー11日到着、公演準備のため4日間で心残りなく使い、15日のアルヘンチーナはアンコールアンコールで最后のアルヘンチーナのカスタネットによる踊りは熱狂そのもので、私もアルヘンチーナの恩恵を、そして頌へることが少しでもあったとよろこびました。16日のナンシー市のレセプションでは私の公演を観て頂いた方々パリ、リヨンの新聞記者を含めて大勢の方々から握手をされ、だきかゝえられました。パリの記者はアルヘンチーナをみていて、私が日本で観、私はそのことによって舞踏を志したと話しました。

第二日16日夜も、拍手がおさえにおさえられ最後に爆発した様な感じで、これまた私にとって最上の落付いた、特に波のラストでは観衆の心にしみて行ったものと私は受取り、受取った感動のはねかえりを感じました。観衆とともに波を感じた次第です。之につづいて「眠りからさめた子供」の一曲半のくり返しにより、フェナーレ［原文ママ］と踊り部分がくりされ［原文ママ］尚多くの續いた拍手に応えて、ラストのラストは上杉さんのスカートを後で後背のようにかゝけ、私がレオ（家に来ていた獨人）から受けたリラの花たばを日本の墓にさゝけるようにさゝけ、次に私が上杉さんの手をとって結婚式のマーチのように退場。この時は練習のとき山添さんが偶然けいこしていたショパンのソナチネ。

　この墓であり、「天と地の結婚」の様な場面は、市川さんが記念に上杉さんを前にし後に男三人がならび楽しんでいたのをみつけ、最

后のフィナーレのまとめとしました。この時も美しさに拍手がたえることなく續き、私も弟子と関りのない所で関り、私の最上のものを展開出来たと信じております。

第二日の朝に、パリから全国放送がアルヘンチーナを絶賛した放送があったと伝えてくれ、夜の公演にはパリの放送局によって「胎児の夢」を、そして二十日にはアルヘンチーナ頌のテレビを撮りに来ることになってます（フィルムは両方共頂けるそうです）。

パリリヨンの記者も共に大変よろこび、駅の構内のような大きな喫茶店（駅前ホールも同じ）に入っても皆よろこんで迎えていてくれている様で、拍手やら手をふってくれます。

NANCY到着后、教会を訪ね私の舞踏家としての証しと願いを受け入れてくれ、音（パイプオルガン）の打合わせもすみ、20午后に1時間程度立ちます。

盲目のオルガニストと。

3、400年位前らしいです。古い教会で、入っていったらお葬式をやっていました　翌日たね［原文ママ］にオルガンを弾いてくれましたが、私は最初、二階で演奏、私は壇の奥まった所に立っていましたが、今迄経験した事のない私の心のうちがいつの間にか私を動かし、極めて自然に、何が経験した事のない世界へ一歩ふみ出した様な感じでした。私はやはり来てよかった。教会で立つことが出来るよろこびを心から感じています。

牧師さんが第一日に観にこられ、長いよろこびと感動の手紙を頂き、チャイルドとゆう言葉

en plein ciel, le

ナンシー到着公演準備のため 4日間心残りなく使い 15日の
アルヘンチーナはアンコールアンコールで最後のアルヘンチーナのカスタネット
による踊りは熱狂そのもので私もアルヘンチーナの恩恵をそれに与ることが
少しもあったとよろこびました。16日のナンシー市のレセプションでは私の
公演を観て下さった方々 パリ、リヨンの新聞記者を含めて大勢の
方々から握手をされだきがえられました パリの記者はアルヘンチーナ
をみていて 私が日本で親永なえのことによって舞踊を志したと注しました
又16日夜も拍手がおさえにおさえられ最後に爆発した様な感じで
これ又私にとって最上の踊付いた。昔の波のラストでは観衆の心にしみ
て踊ったものと私は受取り 受取った感動のはねかえりを感じました
観衆と共に波を感じた次第です それにつづいて眠りからさめた子鳥の
一曲半のくり返しによりフィナーレと踊り部分がすされ 尚多くの
続いた拍手に応えて

ラストのラストは

上杉さんのスカートを後で 後背なるふかしげ 私がレオ(婦人)
から受けたりうの靴などを暮らんにさけるよるにさけ 次に私が上杉
さんの手をとって 結婚式のマーチのように亜坊 この時は練習の時
市添さんが偶然けにいしていた ショパンのソナタえ
この墓でおり天と地の結婚の様な場面は市川さんが記念に上杉さん
をおし 後に男三人がならび 楽しんでいたのをみつけ最後のフィナーレ
のまとめとしました この時も美しさに拍手が応えることなく僕等私も
弟子(寄りのない所で)(寄り 私の最上のものを) 尾南主未定に信じております
又二日の朝にパリから金口放送がアルヘンチーナと絶賛した放送が
あったと伝えてくれ 夜の公演にはパリの放送局にて脇兄の暮を
をし 二十日にはアルヘンチーナ同のテレビーを撮りに来ることになってます
パリの記者も共に大変するこびに 大ぷさ契葉店(写杉 ポも同じ)
写事の橋内のような

を使い祝福して下さいました。ナンシーとパリの教会で証することになってます。
身体は仕上げまで大変でしたが、腰もいたくなくバランスも私なりに完璧な様に［原文ママ］状態です。波の前のバッハおどれました。
ナンシーから一時間はなれた所で（ストラスブルグ）でアルヘンチーナ頌、パリでは4、5、6の3日間の予定が加わり、その后のパリの追加公演はことわるより外ないと市川さんは押えています
夏のカナダの公演の後訪ねる予定の竹井恵が、マネジャをつれて観に来てくれましたが、市川さんの配慮によるものと、ニューヨークを訪ねた時に公演を望んでおりましたので　よろこんでいます。
女性群男性群皆元気です。そして私を大事にしてくれチームワークに満点です。沢氏が佛語（フランス）出来て、照明のチーフは尊敬して協力してくれ、沢氏はチーフだと言ってます。美しい円型のオペラハウスで照明は現代的でありませんが、在る道具を用い最大によい照明が出来ているようで、舞台かんとく中村、照明池部、秀島さんはその間にあってよい運営がなされています。
専任のつきそいの人が3人もつき、日本人の通譯（つうやく）又リヨンから丸紅の通譯も協力してくれ、アナウンス等遺感ありません。
鎌倉の奥さんの御恢復（ごかいふく）をいつも祈っております。
少しでもいたみがすくなく御恢復を祈るのみです。
心の中に祈りつゝ、最大の努力をつづけることが出来、私は感謝してます。

お母さん
元気ですが夜おそかったので今夜は少し早く週に一回ぐらい連絡します　慶人とも直接話出来たらと想いますがとにかく元気ですから安心して下さい　あなたもくれぐれ注意しなが子供等お願いします

けいこちゃん
おげんきですか　みんなのしゃしんを持って（も）来なかったのでさびしいです　ごはんだけでなくおしょうゆをかけておいしくお肉（にく）　お魚（さかな）やさい　なんでもだんだんたべられるようになってよかったですね　おちいちゃは大きなめだまをぎょろぎょろさして　おかしやをのぞき　お人形さんはどれがいいかきをつけていますよ

はるちゃん
おねえちゃん
私は年を忘れて　年を越えて　元氣でやってます
おみやげを忘れずに
ミニカー
おねえちゃんには上杉さんに注意してみてもらってます
二人共おくれないでね？
ではこれで

ピアニストの山添さんも一生懸命でフランス語もよく話します

052

053

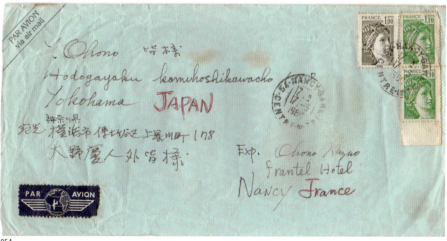
054

Letters from Kazuo Ohno

A letter from Nancy

I arrived in Nancy (on the 11th). I availed of the four days to prepare for performance without hesitation. At [the performance of] *La Argentina* on the 15th [the audience] was so excited that they called out *encore, encore* whereupon I enthusiastically danced to the [recording of] La Argentina's castanets, I could also benefit from [the presence] of Argentina, and there was also a sense of celebration.

Many of those who saw the performance, including newspaper reporters from Paris and Lyon, attended the public reception hosted by Nancy City on the 16th where I was greeted with handshakes and hugs. I told those reporters who had seen Argentina perform in Paris that I, too, had seen her perform in Japan and that was what ultimately induced me to becoming a dancer.

On the second day, on the evening of the 16th, while the applause was [initially] suppressed, it felt as though it erupted at the end. Particularly at the end of the scene with the wave, I felt the audience's utmost calm and the repercussions of the emotions that penetrated their hearts. After the section with the wave, [Liszt's] *Hymne de l'enfant à son réveil* was repeated one and a half times; we performed the finale and repeated the dance. In response to the subsequent applause at the very end, I held the back of Uesugi-san's skirt as if it were an aura and as though offering the bunch of lilac blossoms I received from Leo (the German guy who came to my home) to a (Japanese) grave, I then took Uesugi san's hand and exited the stage as though [performing] a wedding march. At the moment [I used] Chopin's *Sonatine* that Yamazoe-san had unexpectedly rehearsed. As a

tribute to Ichikawa-san, the finale came to an end with this graveyard-like scene reminiscent of *The Marriage of Heaven and Earth*, with Uesugi-san at the front while three male [dancers] were lined up behind enjoying themselves. This scene was so beautiful that the applause didn't stop. [It then dawned on me] that I could perform with my students in unexpected places and I believe that I was able to express my innermost self.

On the morning of the second day, I was told that a programme by a national broadcaster from Paris had praised *La Argentina*. That evening a Parisian broadcaster shot *The Dream of the Foetus*, and on the 20th, they are to come to shoot *Admiring La Argentina* for TV (we are told that we will receive [footage] from both films). The journalists from Paris and Lyon are also extremely delighted. Even if we enter a café (as large as a station) everyone warmly greets us, applauding and shaking our hands (The same goes for the hall in front of the station).

After arriving in Nancy, I visited the church where my testimony and yearning as a dancer [to perform there] was accepted. A consultation for the music (pipe organ) was also held. I will perform there for about one hour on the 20th with a blind organist. It seems to be about three or four hundred years old. As I entered the old church, a funeral was being held. I stood at the back of the pulpit while the organ was being played up in the balcony. All of a sudden my heart felt something I never before experienced, something that moved me. I felt as though I was stepping into a world I'd never experienced in an extremely natural way.

I'm glad I came here after all. I truly feel the joy of being able to perform in a church.

The priest came on the first day to see [my performance] and I received a long joyful and passionate letter [from him]. He blessed me using the word "child." I will be able to testify [to my faith] in churches in Nancy and in Paris. Physically, it was hard to prepare everything, but my hips don't hurt and my balance, in typical fashion, is in perfect condition. I could dance to Bach before the scene with the wave.

I will perform *Admiring La Argentina* in a city about one hour away from Nancy (Strasburg).

In Paris, three days, the 4th, 5th, and 6th will be added to the schedule.

Ichikawa-san is of the opinion that we should turn down any additional performances in Paris after that. Kei Takei, whom I was supposed to visit after this summer's performance in Canada, came to see my performance with her manager. I am grateful to Ichikawa-san for having arranged this and I'm glad to know that she wishes me to perform in New York.

The group of women and men are all doing well, taking good care of me and their teamwork is tops.

Sawa-san can speak French. The chief of lighting respects me and is helpful and claims that Sawa-san is [good enough to be] the chief. While the lighting in a beautiful circular opera house is not modern, it seems as though the best lighting is made using existing tools. Everything has panned out well with Nakamura as stage director, Ikebe as lighting operator; and Hideshima [helping out] in between.

I'm assisted by three attendants, as well as a Japanese interpreter and Marubeni's interpreter from Lyon. I am happy with how they go about their work.

I'm constantly praying for the recovery of the lady [Osaragi-san] in Kamakura.

If she could just suffer a little less, I pray for her recovery.

I'm praying in my heart. I am grateful that I'm able to continue my utmost efforts.

My dear wife, I'm doing fine, but I'm [usually finished] late at night, so tonight [I'm] a little earlier

I'll be in touch once a week. I'd thought to talk to Yoshito directly, but anyway

please rest assured that I'm doing fine. Take good care of yourself and the children.

Keiko-chan

How are you? I'm lonely because I didn't bring everyone's photo along.

I'm happy that you are gradually eating all kinds of food, not only rice, but also meat, fish and vegetables with soy sauce.

Grandpa's eyes are wide open, looking to find delicious sweets in the pastry shops and cute dolls for you.

Haru-chan, Onee-chan

I've forgotten my age and doing much better than my years.

I won't forget the souvenirs

A minicar

Uesugi-san is looking out for them for Onee-chan

You won't be late, won't you?

That's it for now.

The Pianist Yamazoe is doing his best and speaks French well.

インタビュー2
天野 功

急所をはずさないという思いを私は大野先生か
ら聞いたような気もするんだけと、要するに、割
合に自由な世界っていうかな、キリスト教の世界
だけが先生の世界ではなくて、途方もなく大きな
舞踏の世界を持ってらっしゃって、そこでの人脈
とか、そこでの先生との触れ合いを持ってる世
界があって、それで生きてる人達が沢山いるわ
けよね。だけとも、先生自身の根っこのところを
見ていくと、キリスト教が脈々として先生を動かし
ているというか、そういう思いがしますね。

大野先生のことを思い出すと、その時の舞踏を
していらっしゃる姿というのが今もありありとこう、
思い起こすんですね。それから、海外に公演に
でかけるようなときはね、ドイツでこうだったとか、
フランスでこうだったとか、というような話をね、
聞かせていただいて、いろんな話を、お土産話
をたくさん聞いたんですよ。で、その中でね、「イ
エスの招き」というね、テーマをね、私から先生
に提案したことがあったんですよね。イエスの招
きというのはね、イエス様との関係というかな、そ
ういうものが信仰の中心にあるはずなんですよっ
ていうことをね、イエス様との関わりを、舞踏で表
現するとどういうことになるでしょうかっていうよう
な話をね、先生からも聞いたり、私からも話をし
たりして、なんとなくね、その「イエスの招き」って
いう舞踏のね、テーマの始まりのところ、根っこの
ところで、ちょっと私のサジェスチョンをさせてい
ただいたことがあったんですね。

先生自身はそれをずっとあたためて、舞踏のひと
つの公演につくりあげたいきさつがあって、そうい
うものをね、この本を見たり、ま、いろんな本を見
たりして深く知ることができるようになったんです

けど、発端っていうかな、そのきっかけっていうの
がね、私とのおしゃべりがきっかけだったんじゃ
ないかなというふうに、私は思っているんですね。

カトリックの教会の、礼拝堂の中で、マリアの像と、
イエスを抱いているマリアの像と両方あって、そ
のイエスを抱いているマリアの像の、イエスの足
を、先生がこう、なんかで、ええ、お花で触れたと
かって、そういうことで先生のほうからイエス様の
足に触れるというようなね、ひとつの場面があっ
たんだという話を聞いて、うん、それは、そういう
ことはあるだろうなと思ったんです、私は。イエス
様が私達を呼んでいるんですっていうね、だから、
逆の立場で、イエス様の招きを聴く、受ける、そし
て近づいていくというようなね、能動的な、イエス
様に近づく私達の信仰というものがあるんじゃな
いでしょうかっていう話をしたと思うんですね。そ
れがまあ、この「イエスの招き」の中でね、実現
してきた。「イエスの招き」っていう舞踏は、私も
何回か見せていただいたんですけど、それがね、
深く、先生の舞踏の中で展開して、素晴らしい
作品になったんじゃないかなというふうに思った。
2016.5.5

天野 功｜元捜真バプテスト教会牧師（1974年〜2002
年）。大野一雄、大野チエは教会の信徒だった。

INTERVIEW 2

Isao Amano

I recall hearing Ohno-sensei talking about the importance of not overlooking what is vital. His world was freer and was not confined to Christianity, for it also embraced the vast world of Butoh. In terms of personal relationships, he could create a rapport with many others through Butoh. And yet, if I examine the roots of Sensei's character, I feel as though Christianity was a vital force for him.

Whenever I think of Ohno-sensei, I can still see his Butoh performance on that day [of his wife's funeral service]. On returning from his tours to France or Germany and elsewhere, he would fill me in on his travels and all about his performances. One of them was *An Invitation to Jesus*, a theme I had suggested to him. "An Invitation to Jesus" is about our relationship with Jesus. I taught him that this relationship should be at the core of our faith. And we talked about expressing this relationship with Jesus through Butoh. It was a two-way discussion between Sensei and I. The original inspiration for his Butoh performance *An Invitation to Jesus* came about as a result of a suggestion I made to him, I believe.

Ohno-sensei nurtured this theme for a long time and afterwards created a Butoh performance. I read this and many other books and got a deeper understanding of him. But I can't help thinking that our discussions were the genesis or the trigger for that performance.

In Catholic chapels one can see statues of the Virgin Mary and of Mary holding the infant Jesus. I heard that Sensei once touched the foot of Jesus on a statue of Mary with flowers. Sensei approached Jesus to touch his foot in such a way. When he told me about that scene I felt as though Jesus was summoning us. So, inversely, we are hearing Jesus's invitation, accept it, and get closer to him. We talked about how there can be such faith that we actively approach Jesus. Sensei embodies this faith in *An Invitation to Jesus*. I had the opportunity to watch this piece on several occasions. He had deeply developed this theme in his Butoh to create a wonderful piece.

May 5, 2016

Isao Amano Pastor at Soshin Baptist Church (1974-2002). Both Kazuo Ohno and his wife Chie Ohno were members of the congregation.

100歳
Centenary Birthday

2006年10月に満百歳になった。体力が衰えても、踊りたい気持ちは変わらなかった。家族と研究生がいつもそばにいた。

In October 2006, Kazuo Ohno turned one hundred. Even though his physical strength was on the wane, his desire to perform remained as strong as ever. His family and students were constantly at his side.

055

055. 2005年頃
Circa 2005, surrounded by carers and students.

056.

057.

056. 2002年頃｜自宅の食卓でも踊る
Circa 2002, Dancing at the dinner table at home.

057. 2001年｜自宅にて
2001, At home.

058.

059.

058. 2000年代｜調子の良い日は、稽古にも参加した｜撮影：吉田隆一
2000s, on his good days, Ohno participated in practice session. photo: Lieuichi Yoshida

059. 2002年｜大地の芸術祭越後妻有アートトリエンナーレ｜舞い落ちるチューリップの中で｜中央にいけばな作家 中川幸夫
2002, with Yukio Nakagawa, the Ikebana master, at their joint performance featuring tulip petals at the Echigo Tsumari Art Triennale．

61

060. 2002年｜座って手だけで踊る｜撮影：宮田均
Ohno in his chair, dancing just with his hands. photo: Hitoshi Miyata

061.

062.

061. 2002年｜釧路のジャズ喫茶ジス・イズにて｜撮影：村山信隆
2002, at the Jazz Café, Kushiro. photo: Nobutaka Murayama

062. 2006年｜自室にて｜写真家 細江英公の訪問を受ける
2006, The photographer Eikoh Hosoe visits Ohno.

63

衣装
Costumes

衣装ができたときは踊りができていた。造花の
紙の花は葬儀屋さんでもらってきた。外国に行く
と古着屋で衣装を探した。

Costumes determined his dance; without
one there was not the other. Ohno would
pick up artificial paper flowers at the funeral home. Whenever he travelled overseas,
he would rummage through the local thrift
stores for costumes.

063

064

063-064. 「衣装とは宇宙を羽織ること」｜撮影：神山貞次郎
"A costume dresses the Universe." photo : Teijiro Kamiyama

065.

066.

065. 1986年｜稽古場にて｜撮影：ヌリート・マッソン＝セキネ
1986, In rehearsal at the Kazuo Ohno Dance Studio.
photo : Nourit Masson-Sékiné

066. 1990年｜フィレンツェの楽屋にて
1990, Dressing room Florence.

067

068

067. 1981年｜ニューヨーク、ラ・ママの楽屋にて｜撮影：山口晴久
1981, Dressing room at La Mama, New York. photo : Haruhisa Yamaguchi

068. 1986年｜撮影：会田健一郎
1986, photo: Kenichiro Aita

069.　1987年｜マドリッドの楽屋にて｜撮影：武田幸子
　　　1987, Dressing room Madrid. photo: Sachiko Takeda

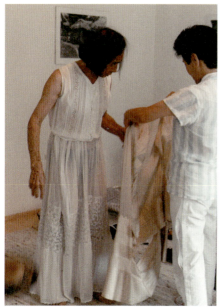
070

071

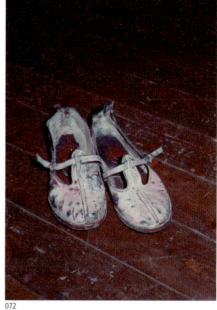
072

070.-071. 1989年｜ウィーンにて｜街で見つけた古着を着てみる｜撮影：アンジェラ・ワルデック
1989, Trying on costumes he found in the local thrift stores, Vienna. photo: Angela Waldegg

072. 自分でペンキを何度も塗った
Ohno dyed his own shoes.

69

073.

074.

073. 1986年｜『ラ・アルヘンチーナ頌』最後の場面の衣装｜撮影：会田健一郎
 1986, Costume for the finale of *Admiring La Argentina*. photo: Kenichiro Aita

074. 1987年｜イスラエルの美術家 ヌリートの個展にて｜撮影：ヌリート・マッソン＝セキネ
 1987, At Nourit Masson-Sékiné's solo exhibition. photo: Nourit Masson-Sékiné

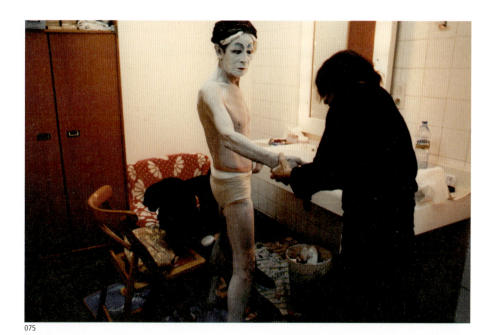
075.

076.

075. 1987年｜顔の化粧をして体を白く塗る｜撮影：武田幸子
 1987, Applying shiro-nuri to his body.
 photo: Sachiko Takeda

076. 2007年｜ボローニャでの大野一雄展｜色とりどりの帽子
 ｜撮影：ルチア・バルディーニ
 2007, An assortment of Ohno's hats exhibited at
 Bologna's museum. photo: Lucia Baldini

71

アントニア・メルセ
Antonia Mercé,
a.k.a. La Argentina

学生時代に帝国劇場で来日公演を見た。「ラ・
アルヘンチーナ頌」をパリで上演したときは、ア
ントニア・メルセの姪の家に招かれた。郊外にあ
る墓にも詣でた。

As a student, Ohno saw La Argentina
perform in at Tokyo's Imperial Theater.
When he performed *Admiring La Argentina*
in Paris, he was invited to Mercé's niece's
home. Ohno also visited her grave in the
Parisian suburbs.

077.　レコードジャケット｜カスタネットの女王と呼ばれた｜撮影:佐々木悦久
　　　Record sleeve, Argentina was known as the Queen of Castanets.　photo: Yoshihisa Sasaki

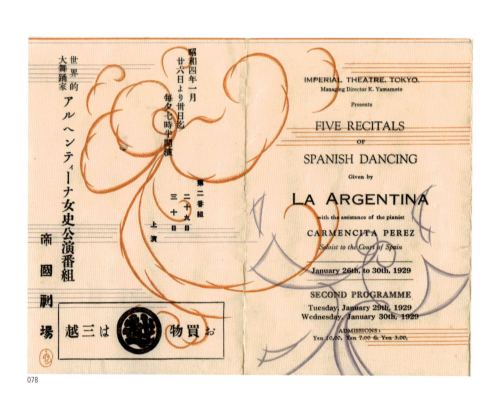

078. 1929年帝国劇場公演プログラム
Program for her performance at Tokyo's Imperial Theatre 1929.

079. 大野一雄は22歳、3階席から公演を見た
At 22, Ohno watched La Argentina perform from the third floor.

080

081

082

083

080-082. 1980年｜パリにて｜アントニア・メルセの姪 カルロッタの家に招かれた｜撮影：佐々木悦久
1980, Ohno visited La Argentina's niece Carlotta during his visit to Paris.
photo: Yoshihisa Sasaki

083. アントニアのケープをプレゼントされた
Ohno was presented with one of La Argentina's capes.

084.

085.

086.

084. アントニア・メルセの像の前で｜撮影：佐々木悦久
Beside a bust of La Argentina.
photo: Yoshihisa Sasaki

085. アントニア・メルセ（1890〜1936）
Antonia Mercé (1890-1936)

086. アルバムを贈られた｜撮影：佐々木悦久
Looking through La Argentina's photo albums.
photo: Yoshihisa Sasaki

77

087

088

087.-088.　1982年｜バルセロナで再会
1982, Reunion with Carlotta in Barcelona.

089

090

089.-090.　1986年｜パリ郊外 ヌイイにある墓に詣でる
　　　　　1986, Visiting La Argentina's grave in Neuilly.

79

インタビュー 3

中島昭子

とにかくよく歩かれるんですよ、大野先生が。年齢から考えても、私もなるべくご負担が少ないように、ここはメトロにしましょうとか、ここはバスにしましょうとか、ここは先生方、タクシーにしましょうとか、なんとなくアレンジをしながらご案内をするんだけれども、大野先生、どこまでもどこまでも、歩くの。で、まあ正直、私としては、先生はいいかもしれないけど、私はそろそろバスに乗りたいな、みたいに思うんだけど、歩くの。古着屋さんみたいなの、けっこうあるんですよ。レースのショールのようなものとか、昔の貴族のね、マダムがかけてたようなのとか。帽子につける、ちょっとした飾りみたいな、ブローチというよりは、分類は、まあブローチなんでしょうけど、飾りのようなものだとか。まあ、とにかくそれも、よく歩きましたね。そう、クリニャンクールの蚤の市はえらくお気に入りだったんです。

ポンピドゥーセンターっていうのがあるんですよね。あそこの前がちょっとした広場みたいになってるんですね。そこで、まあ、大道芸って言っていいんでしょうか、アコーディオンかバイオリンを弾いている、おじさんがいたんですよ。大野先生よりはちょっと若い。その前に、帽子だか缶からだかが置いてあって、気に入った人はそこに、1フランとか。その音を聴きながら大野先生は、そこのそばに近寄っていって。路上ですよ。いきなり、街頭ライブですよね。いきなり踊りだしちゃったの。あらーってね、ビックリしましたよね。私なんかはその、どうしていいかわからない。一緒にいた方達に、「いいんですか?」って言ったら、「いや、こういう方ですから」。

我々は遠巻きにっていうかね。大野先生がその横で踊られるのを、見てたわけです。そしたら、何分ぐらい踊ってらしたのかな、気が付いたら黒山の人だかりだった。あらー。さっきまでね、音楽だけのときは誰も、誰もっていうか、ちょっとはいたかもしれませんけど、ほとんど閑散としていたところに、うわーっと人が集まってしまった。踊り終わったら、もう拍手と、それから、さっきまで何かこう少ししかお金が入ってなかったところが、こんなに。その弾いてた方が、演奏者の方が何かおっしゃってるんだけど、大野先生が「ん?」っていう感じで。私がしょうがないから、しょうがないっていうか、まあ行って、何ですか?って言ったら、これは山分けだって言ってくれっていうんですね。大野先生に、こちらの方が、先生、このあれ、山分けだっておっしゃってますけどって言ったら、大野先生がまた、あの、優雅な仕草で、全部、こちらの彼の方にすーっと押したんですね。そして、ありがとうっておっしゃって。まあ、ありがとうぐらいわかるの、向こうの人もね。ありがとうって言われて、深々頭を下げて、まあつまり、これは全部自分のものになり、おまけにありがとうって言ってもらって、すごく嬉しそうにして。そして、大野先生、また何事もなかったかのように、延々とパリの街を歩くんですよ。

2016.4.19

中島昭子 | 捜真学院学院長。大野一雄の教え子。
1980年の初のパリ公演では通訳を務めた。

INTERVIEW 3
Akiko Nakajima

Ohno-sensei used to walk everywhere. Considering his age, I advised him and his companions to take the metro or the bus. Or, I would make arrangements for him to take a taxi, but nonetheless he walked everywhere. To be frank, whatever about Sensei, I felt like riding the bus after some time, but he walked. He would rummage through antique clothing stores, trying out lace shawls that were worn by aristocratic ladies. He would try on a hat with a brooch or those ornaments one puts in hats. He walked from one store to the next. He really enjoyed the flea market at Clignancourt.

There's a small plaza in front of the Pompidou Centre where a street performer on accordion or violin was busking. He was a little younger than Sensei and had a hat and a tin with which to collect money from passers-by. On hearing the music, Ohno-sensei started heading in his direction and suddenly dancing right there on the spot. I was gobsmacked and didn't know what to do. I asked Sensei's companions. They told me not to worry, for that was his style.
As we stood at some distance and watched him dance, a large crowd suddenly gathered to watch. Hardly anyone had been paying any attention when the musician was playing by himself. And yet, a crowd gathered as soon as Ohno-sensei started to perform. After he stopped dancing the crowd applauded and the busker's hat was now full. The musician started speaking with Ohno-sensei. Given he couldn't understand what the musician was saying, I went over to interpret. He was pointing out Ohno-sensei's share of the takings. I translated for Sensei that he was to take his share of the takings. Whereupon Ohno-sensei elegantly returned the money. He said "arigatou," deeply bowing his head. The musician could probably understand what that meant. He looked delighted to pocket the entire takings and to be thanked for it to boot. And so, Ohno-sensei continued walking through Paris as though nothing had happened.

April 19, 2016

Akiko Nakajima Director of the Soshin Gakuin. Former student of Kazuo Ohno. She served as Kazuo Ohno's interpreter during his earliest performance in Paris in 1980.

ボイラー室
Boiler Room

教職を退いた後、同じ学校のボイラー室で働くことになった。学校が好きだった。1969年に作った、最初の映画『O氏の肖像』をそこで撮影した。

Such was Ohno's love for the Soshin School, that after retiring from teaching, he decided to continue work as a janitor in the boiler room there. In 1969, *The Portrait of Mr. O*, the first film in the trilogy, was partly shot there.

091.

091. 捜真女学校のボイラー室 「I work last ten years」と裏にある
A snapshot of the boiler at the Soshin Girls' School, on its back Ohno wrote: "I work last ten years."

092

093

094

095

096

097

098

099

100

101

102

103

85

104

105

106

107

108

109

110

111

112

092-112.　1968年頃｜映画『O氏の肖像』撮影の頃｜撮影：ボブ藤崎
　　　　　Circa 1968, Taken around the time making *The Portrait of Mr O*. photo: Bob Fujisaki

インタビュー4

大野美加子

前から、すごく研究熱心だから、おじいちゃんは。常に絵の展覧会に行ったりとか、常にメモしたりとか、あの、その制作、紙。わら半紙にいろいろマジックで書いて、だから、常にマジックと紙とコーヒーと煙草っていうのが、常に。煙草も吸ってましたから、まあ、持ち歩いてた、みたいな。あのピースのこういう缶。基本的に、昔の話は、戦争の話とか、そういうことはほとんどしないですね。聞いてもしない。だから、あんまり話さない。黙ってる。そう、それで、だからいつも何か書いて。あとは、教会で説教するための原稿を書いてたりも。だいたい毎週行ってましたね。座る席も決まってみたいだし、うん。毎週、捜真教会か、たまに上星川教会、うん。まあそれで、教会でも幼稚園でもサンタクロースやるときも、長靴を買ったりとか、そういう準備をしてましたね。仕事としては、学校にも行ったりとかしてたし、後は、普段は草むしりやったりとか、ペンキ塗りやったりとか。ペンキをけっこう得意としてたんじゃないかな、と思うんですけど。だから舞台があっても午前中は草むしりをやるとか、普段の生活は基本的には変えないで舞台に出る、みたいな。どこで踊るのも、基本同じ気持ちでいたんじゃないかなと思いますね。小さいところであろうが、大きいところであろうが、一人でも自分のことを見てくれる人がいるから、僕は行くんだっていう感じで。

『睡蓮』とか『花鳥風月』とか、大野一雄と大野慶人が一緒に踊る舞台のときは、大変でしたよね、家の中は。「お前舞台に出るのか、出ないのか」みたいな。「俺は嫌だ」みたいな。「出てくれなきゃ困るんだ」みたいな、そういう二人の葛藤が、結構、うん、喧嘩みたいな話合いで。まあ、そのアルヘンチーナつくるときも、土方さんが、ああじゃ

ない、こうじゃないとか。そういうことを言う人っていうのが家の中であんまりいなかったから、結構、この人怖い、みたいな、土方さんに対して。まあ、おじいちゃんに対してモノを言うっていう人があんまりいなかったんで、土方さんは、もっとこうして、みたいなことがあったから、ああ、この人怖いのかな、なんてちょっと思いましたね。

ツアーでは、おじいちゃんと二人の部屋でずーっと過ごしてましたけど、ま、別に、静かな感じで、普通に朝ご飯を食べて、で、お昼になったら劇場に行って、まあ、普通に。特に何の会話をするわけでもなく、普段の、家にいるのと同じように過ごしてたような気がします。一番最初に行ったのは、イタリアのパルマ。パルマに行きました。その時は、おじいちゃんと父と母と私と4人で行って、よくやってきたなぁと思いますよね。パルマに行って、その後、どこかへ行ってますよね。ローマ？　そうですね、ミラノも行ったし、ローマも行って、そう、コモ。あれが最初ですかね。まあ、反応はよかったですよね、お客さんも入ってたし。大野一雄は結構、興奮して舞台やってましたね。曲が終わってるのに終わってないと思ってたりとか、けっこう、着替えるときもわりと焦ってたし、ああ、気持ちが昂ってるなっていうのは感じましたけど、お客さんは喜んでくれたかなぁと。

2016.11.25

大野美加子｜大野慶人長女。ツアーでは衣装を担当。幼い頃、大野一雄主演映画『O氏の肖像』に出演している。

INTERVIEW 4

Mikako Ohno

Grandpa had always been very studious and regularly went to art exhibitions and such. He always had rough-paper and a marker on which he would jot down notes. He always had a marker and paper, coffee, and cigarettes to hand. He used to smoke and always carried a tin of Peace cigarettes around with him. He never spoke about the past or the war, even if we asked him. He rarely spoke; he remained quiet. Instead, he was constantly writing something down. He would also draft sermons for the church. He would go to church almost every week and had his own pew. He would usually go to Soshin Baptist Church or occasionally to Kamihoshikawa Church. Whenever he went to the church or to the Kindergarden or to play Santa Claus, he was well-prepared; he bought rain boots for the Santa Claus role. He also worked at the school and did housework such as weeding and painting. Actually he was pretty good at painting. He was constantly busy between painting and weeding, so that even on performance days he would weed the garden in the morning. Basically, his lifestyle didn't change. Irrespective of where he was dancing, whether at a small or a large venue, he was ready to dance even for an audience of one person.

At home the preparation process was quite problematic, especially for performances such as *Water Lilies* in which both grandpa and my father were to perform together. It was tough going. There was a lot of deliberation about whether my father [Yoshito] would dance or not. Grandpa kept pressurising him to perform. Their discussions were pretty argumentative. Hijikata-san was present when grandpa was rehearsing *Admiring La Argentina* and would constantly give him advice. At home nobody could speak to him in that manner. I myself was quite fearful of Hijikata-san. Nobody ever stood up to grandpa, but Hijikata-san was quite strict with him at times. I recall being afraid of him.

While on tour, I used to share a double room with grandpa. He was very quiet and would eat his breakfast as per usual before we would go to the theatre around midday. We didn't converse that much. It was just as if we were at home together. My first overseas tour was to Italy, to Parma. Just the four of us: my father and mother, grandpa and I. Given the circumstances, I'm still astounded at how well we coped. We went to Parma and later to Rome. We also went to Milan and Como. In retrospect, it was quite something. The audience response was good and he played to full houses. Grandpa became very excited when it came to appearing on stage. He would continue dancing even after the music stopped and he was quite anxious when he was changing costumes. I could feel his emotional upsurge, but audiences enjoyed the performance, I believe.

November 25, 2016

Mikako Ohno Yoshito Ohno's eldest daughter. She was in charge of costumes during his overseas tours. As a child, she appeared in the film *The Portrait of Mr. O* featuring Kazuo Ohno.

聖劇
The Nativity Play

教員として勤務していた捜真女学校で生徒達の
聖劇を指導し、自らも出演した。教壇を退き営
繕職になってからも、退職してからも、さらに車
椅子になってからも続いた。

Ohno taught the Nativity play to students
at Soshin Girls' School, where he worked as
a teacher, and he himself also made an
appearance. This tradition continued well
after his retirement from teaching; he
participated in the yearly play even after he
stopped working as a janitor and later when
he was confined to a wheelchair.

113

114

113.-114.　ミッションスクールで聖劇の指導を始めた、毎年のクリスマスの中心行事だった
　　　　　Under Ohno's guidance the Nativity Play was an annual Christmas event at the Mission School.

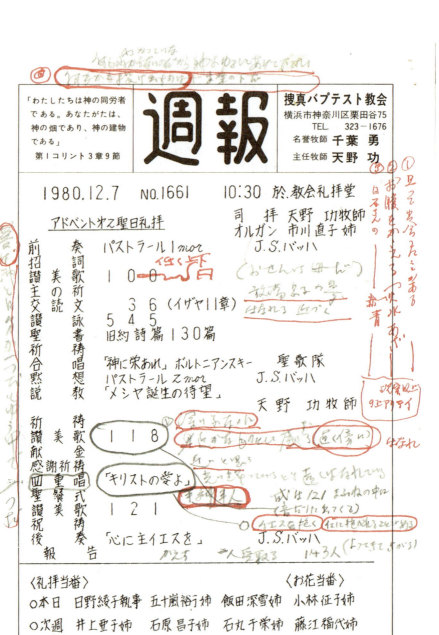

115. 1980年12月7日｜通っていた捜真バプテスト教会の週報に踊りのアイディアを書き込んでいる
Ohno penned some ideas about dance in the Soshin Baptist Church's bulletin on 7 December 1980.

116. 中央の書き込みは「地上の石けり（上杉）　大木に身をすりよせて息子のために祈った　胎児の夢を今実現しているのでなかろうか　おそろしさを感じた　子供はまねをする　上杉さんは石けり（大人）　医者は出来るが母にはこれより出来ない　狂気とはこうゆうことか」

Ohno wrote : "Hopscotch on the ground (Uesugi)

Praying for the son, while physically attached to the large tree. *The Dream of the Foetus* has now been realized. I felt horror. The child imitates . Uesugi-san [playing] at hopscotch (adult). While I'm able to play the doctor, but am unable to go any further with the mother. What is madness?"

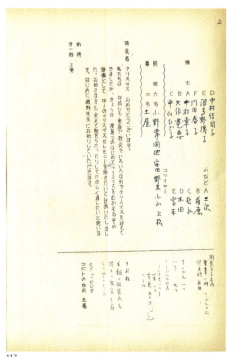
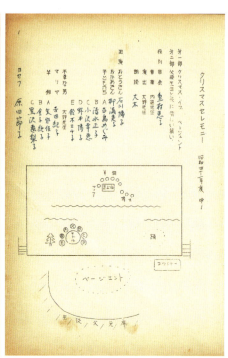

117. 1966年の台本｜15分ほどの聖劇の演出に全力を注いだ
　　　Script for the 1966 version. Ohno invested himself fully for the fifteen-minute Nativity Play.

118.

119.

118.	自らが聖母マリアとなり踊ることもあった	119.	1983年
	Ohno also danced the Virgin Mary.		1983 performance.

95

120.　1998年｜捜真教会クリスマス礼拝｜撮影：竹内北子
　　　1998, Christmas Ceremony at Soshin Baptist Church. photo: Kitako Takeuchi

121.

122.

121. 1998年｜撮影：竹内北子
 1998, photo: Kitako Takeuchi

122. 2002年｜車椅子でも参加した
 2002, Ohno even participated when wheelchair bound.

ラ・アルヘンチーナ頌
Admiring La Argentina

ラ・アルヘンチーナ・アントニア・メルセに出会って47年ののち、彼女を讃える作品を創ることができた。71歳のときだった。

At the age of seventy-one, some forty-seven years after his encounter with La Argentina Antonia Mercé, Ohno created an homage to her.

123.
123. 1977年｜初演に向けての稽古風景｜撮影：岡村透純
1977, Rehearsals for premiere. photo: Tojun Okamura

99

124

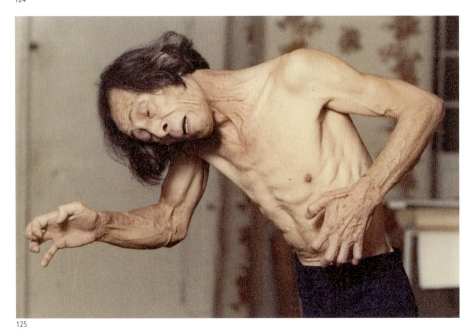
125

124-125.　1977年｜「日常の糧」の場面の稽古を繰り返し行った｜撮影：岡村透純
　　　　　1977, Rehearsing *Daily Bread*.　photo: Tojun Okamura

126.

127.

126. 1977年｜横浜の彫師 彫錦の突然の来訪、作品に緊張をもたらすための稽古
1977, Unexpected visit from the Yokohama tattooist Horikin. Rehearsals in order to introduce tension into the piece.

127. 帝国劇場公演へ連れて行ってくれた恩人、門田義雄氏宅を訪ねて踊る　氏は病の床にあった
Ohno dances on the floor for Yoshio Monden, who had accompanied him to La Argentina's Tokyo performance.

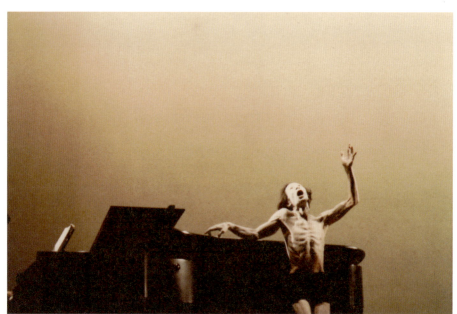

128.

129.

128. 「天と地の結婚」バッハの平均律で踊る
Dancing *The Marriage of Heaven and Earth* to Bach's *The Well Tempered Clavier*.

129. 土方巽の花束を受ける
Receiving a bouquet of flowers from Tatsumi Hijikata.

130.

131.

132.

130. 舞踏家たちとのフィナーレ
   Butoh group finale.

131-132. 終演後の楽屋
   Dressing room after the performance.

133. 冒頭の場面「死と誕生」
The opening section of *Death and Birth*.

134.

135.

134. 1987年｜客席から登場する　開演直前、マドリッドの劇場にて｜撮影：武田幸子
1987, On his way from the dressing room to the auditorium, Madrid. photo: Sachiko Takeda

135. 1982年｜中西夏之の絵画に触発されて作品制作に向かった｜撮影：高田宏
1982, Ohno with Natsuyuki Nakanishi's painting that inspired *Admiring La Argentina*. photo: Hiroshi Takada

105

インタビュー5

大野悦子

作品を見ているというより、踊りそのものを見てる
よね。いい、心に響くような踊りをするかしないかっ
て。作品はあまり関係ない。物語性が全然ない
し。踊ってるときに、いいか悪いかだけ。大野一
雄は、もうどこ行っても踊るから、ヒヤヒヤしてね、
私。自分でほら、どこ行っても、パーティでも、言
われなくても踊るでしょ。迷惑なんじゃないかと思っ
てね、いつもそれはヒヤヒヤしてたわね。

要するに普通の、一般的な話はしないね。踊り
の話ばっかしよね。戦争の話なんか聞きたいか
ら聞くと…私なんかは戦ったものを聞きたいわけ
よ。部下を助けたとか、そういう話はするけどね、
本当にそういう(戦った)話はしてくれなかったね。
だけど、行李にお金がいっぱいあったっていうの
は聞いた。話してた。いくらでもお金は使えたん
だって言ってた。それからやっぱりお父さんがよ
かったのはね、庭いじりよ。草むしり。あれは基
本にあるんじゃない、踊りの基本に。樹をやった
りね、あの庭のね。あれで一日3時間くらいやる
でしょ。あれで勉強してたんだと思う、私。

一回ね、私、お父さんに、ピアノで立つじゃない、
アルヘンチーナの。その時にね、「お父さん、そこ、
磔刑」。ね？　「磔刑みたいに立たなきゃだめよ」
とかなんとか言ったのよ。とっても言葉悪いから
ね、私。そしたらね、お父さん怒ってね、「磔刑っ
てなんだ」って言うのよ。「お父さん、知らないの、
そんなこと」って、喧嘩したことある。一度だけね。
「キリストのこうやってなるのよ」って言って。「キ
リストにならなきゃ、しょうがないじゃないよ」って言っ
て。「十字架にかかってるんだから」って。お父
さん、怒ったね。怒ったことないわね、でも。その
時はね、怒ったっていうより、言葉がきつかった。

だから、私なんかに言われるのが絶対に嫌なの
よね。だんだん、だんだん、ちゃんと聞いてくれる
ようになったけど、あの頃はまだ、お父さんも若い
から、そんなこと言われて批判されるのは嫌なん
じゃない?だけど。(私は)ストレートに言うでしょ。

私は一時期ね、そんな衰えたんだったら踊らない
ほうがいいんじゃないのって言ったことがあった
んですけどね。それは間違いだったわね、私の。
踊ってよかった。死ぬまで踊れたから、いいんじゃ
ない?　ね。やっぱり、ちゃんと魂に響いてくるかな。
土方さんの踊りにはないね。ちょっと、こんなこと。
それはちょっとまずいわね、今の。そういう感動は
ない、土方さんの踊りには。なにがこうしてああ
してこうしてっていう、ひとつの形で訴えてくる。
大野一雄とは全然違うわけよ、訴え方が。だから、
そういう感動は土方さんにはないって言うのよ。
だけど、見てて素晴らしいのよ、見てて面白いし、
チクチクって刺さるところはあるわよ。だけど、大
野一雄のあれとはちょっと違う、感動が。

2019.1.14

大野悦子｜大野慶人夫人。大野一雄・慶人の衣装を担
当。公演衣装となった自身の服も多い。

INTERVIEW 5

Etsuko Ohno

When watching Kazuo perform, I focused on his dance and not the performance. For me, what matters is whether it resonates in our hearts. It has nothing to do with a performance that doesn't have a narrative anyway. What really matters is whether the dance is good or bad. I was constantly on edge, for Kazuo Ohno would end up dancing irrespective of the circumstance. He would even dance at a party without being asked. I thought this might be a nuisance, so I was anxious.

He never engaged in normal conversation. All he ever spoke about was dance. I wanted to learn about the combat during the war. But whenever I asked him, he would just talk about how he had helped his subordinates, but never about the fighting. I only learnt there was so much cash in the army baggage and they could spend it how they liked. Another great thing was his garden work. That was one of the pillars of his dance. He worked about three hours a day weeding and tending the trees. I think this helped him with his dance.

Once when he was rehearsing the scene with the piano in *Admiring La Argentina*, I carelessly told him he should assume a crucified pose. He quipped: "What would you know about the crucifixion?" We argued just that once. I showed him the pose and told him to embody Jesus on the cross. For once Kazuo got angry and spoke severely, for he disliked that I would suggest such a thing. What's more, I spoke bluntly to him. Over time he gradually began to listen to others. But back then he was still young and hated to be criticized.

I once told him that he should think about abandoning dance, for he was getting old. That was wrong of me. It was wonderful that he danced until his final moments. For, unlike Hijikata's dance, his dance resonates in our hearts. Oh, I've put my foot in it, haven't I? What I meant to say was that Hijikata's dance didn't have such passion. Hijikata was wonderful to watch, fascinating, and edgy but lacking such passion. Kazuo Ohno's appeal was different; it was emotional.

January 14. 2019

Etsuko Ohno Yoshito Ohno's wife. She was in charge of costumes for both Kazuo and Yoshito Ohno. Much of Etsuko Ohno's private wardrobe later became performance costumes.

107

体育教員
PE Teacher

日本体育会体操学校を卒業し、関東学院で体育教員になった。その後、捜真女学校に転職するに当たり、女子にダンスを教授するためモダンダンスを習い始めた。

After graduating from the Japan Athletic College, Ohno became a PE education teacher at Kanto Gakuin. Later, on moving to Soshin Girls' School, he began learning modern dance in order to teach his pupils dance.

136. 1930年代
Ohno in the 1930s.

137

138

137. 臨海学校の体操
 Teaching PE at summer camp.

138. 運動会のマスゲーム
 Mass Games at athletic meeting.

139

140

141

139.-141.　1930年代 ｜ スポーツは万能だった
Ohno the all-round athlete.

142. 1950年代｜捜真女学校のアルバムから
From the Soshin Girls' School photo album.

143

144

143. 1950年代女学校の体育館でポーズする写真｜左端に大野一雄
 Kneeling on far left, Ohno poses with his students in the 1950s.

144. 1955年｜国民体育大会神奈川大会開会式のマスゲームを振り付けた
 Ohno choreographed the Mass Games for the Kanagawa Athletic Meet in 1955.

モダンダンス
Modern Dance

1931年に石井漠に、1933年から江口隆哉、宮操子に師事した。1949年に東京共立講堂で最初のリサイタル、その後は毎年のように自主公演を重ねた。

In 1931 he studied Baku Ishii, and as of 1933 under Takaya Eguchi and Misako Miya. His debut solo recital took place at the Tokyo Kyoritsu auditorium in 1949, followed by independently produced performances almost on a yearly basis.

145.

145. 1949年「黄色い帽子」
1949, *The Yellow Hat*

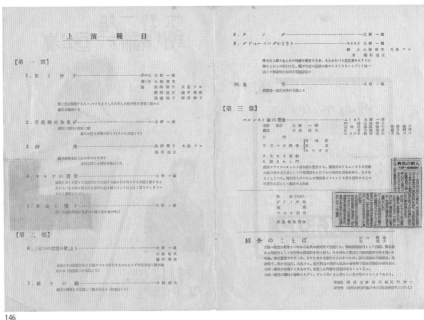

146. 1949年11月｜大野一雄現代舞踊第1回公演プログラム
    Program for Kazuo Ohno's debut dance recital in November 1949.

147. 1950年10月 | 第2回公演プログラム
Program for second recital in October 1950.

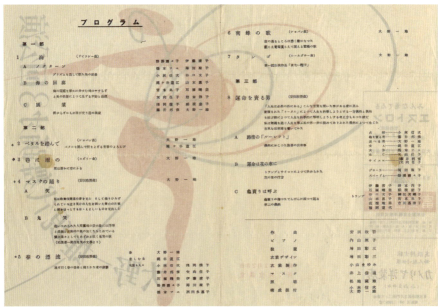

148. 1951年11月｜第3回公演プログラム
Program for third recital in November 1951.

149. 1951年「蜜蜂の歌」
     1951, *Song of the Bees*

150. 1951年「巷に雨の」
     1951, *Downtown Rain*

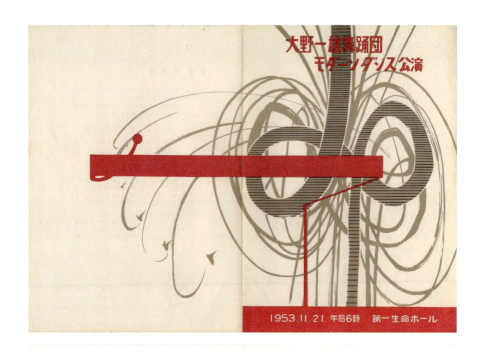

151.

151. 1953年11月、大野一雄舞踊団モダーンダンス公演プログラム
Program for the Kazuo Ohno group's Modern Dance Performance, November 1953.

152

153

154

152. 1953年「天の果実」 高見順の詩より
     1953, *Fruit from Heaven*, from a poem by Jun Takami

154. 1959年「靴」
     1959, *Shoes*

121

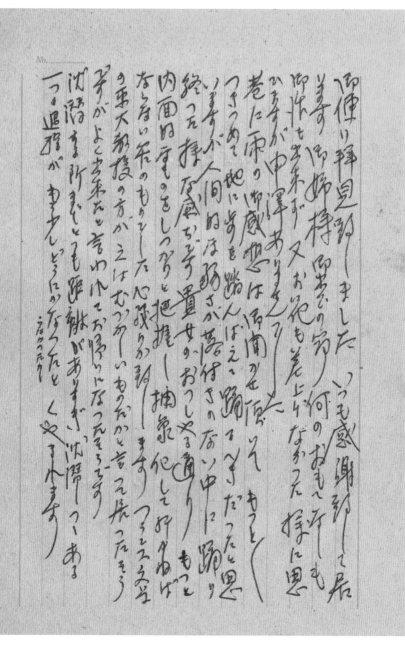

155

155-158. 弟子の山口直永が保管していた
山口直永は前橋女子高等学校で教鞭を執り、「創作ダンスひまわり会」を主宰した
Letter to his student Naoe Yamaguchi. Yamaguchi taught at the Girls High School in Maebashi and was director of the Himawari Creative Dance Group.

大野一雄からの手紙
弟子・山口直永へ

お便り拝見致しました。いつも感謝致しております。お姉様お出での節、何のおもてなしもお話も出来ず、又お花も差上げなかった様に思いますが申訳ありませんでした。

「巷に雨」の御感想は御聞かせ頂いて、もっともっとつきつめて、地に歩を踏んばえて踊るべきだったと思いますが人間的な弱さが落付きのない中に踊り終った様な感じです。貴女がおっしゃる通り、もっと内面的なものをしっかりと把握し抽象化して行かねばならない筈のものでした。心残りが致します。フランス文学の東大教授の方がこれはむづかしいものだがと言っておったそうですがよく出来たと言われてお帰りになったそうです。

沈潜する所までとても距離がありすぎ、沈潜しつつある一つの過程が、もう少しどうにかならなかったかとくやまれます。

色々と解釈批評をいただいてますが見る人により痛い所をつかれますが皆好みがある様で皆好き好きな点を書いておりますが、これまた変った面白い所と思っています。

解釈物足りなさから来る空っぽな気持ちに入りこんだ様な気持ちでしたが、色々と作品を考へ直し取直して今は相等な闘志です。自分の傍に気のつかない秘密があるのだと思うと、でもそれがこの距離が限りなく遠いものでもあると思われます。落付いて勉強し頑張って踊っていい作品をいつか必ず創ります。

種播く人というのを思いうかべ昨年の「春の供物」が、逆に抽象的すぎたというより作心の芯が漠としていたので、此をもっとリアルに内面的なものを表現したいと思ってます。言葉で言い表せず従ってまだ踊るまでには考へを圧縮しなければいけませんが、三つの笑とか、今年のはどうしたらよいか、私はフランス風の場末の風景(劇場)につくり変えようかと思ってます。今年のものはそれなりにもっと圧縮し別に三つの笑を、ユーモラス、悪魔的、狂人と、只こう三つを書くと暗い様なものの字の並びになりますが、明るく取扱いたいと思います。枠をとびぬけた、悪魔的な笑、明るく考えさせられるものを持つ狂人の笑等。

尚、目下ボードレールと取組んで毎晩みんなで持ちよって研究討議しています。人間追及の鮮烈苛烈さの中に、フランス的な香り、モダンな表現(うき上らない)、完全には出来ない事ははっきりしていますが、出来る範囲で。

自分の事ばかり書きましたが、

お身体はどうですか。お元気で明るく静かに養生して下さい。私はどうもいつも此の反対に生活をしているらしい。

短い時でも圧縮された時を。

一度お見舞に参上致したく思って居りますが機会を得たいと思ってます。

どうぞ御身御大事に丈夫になる事に集中する様(自然に出来る)祈ります。

踊りの写真、適当なのがないのでそのうち撮りますから時間が少しかかりますが、それまで小さい私の写真をお送りします。

お大事に。

お姉様によろしくよろしく。

よきクリスマスを迎へられます様。

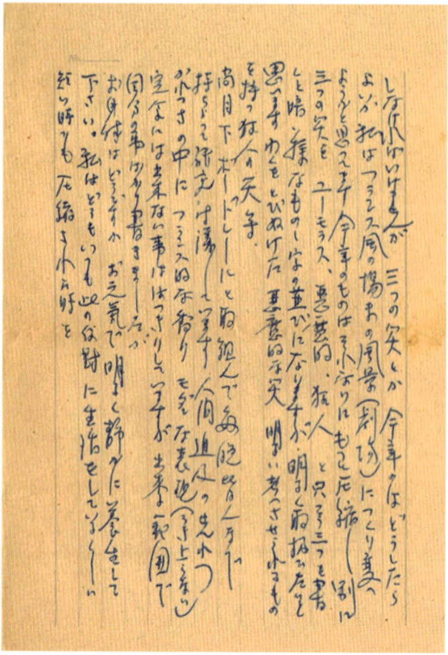

156

157

158

よい　クリスマスを迎へられます様

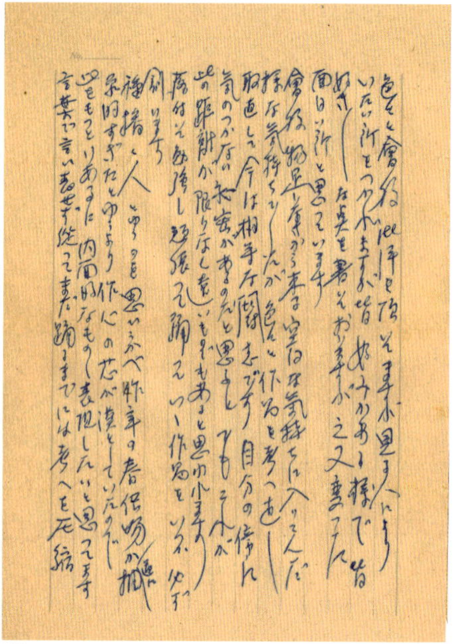

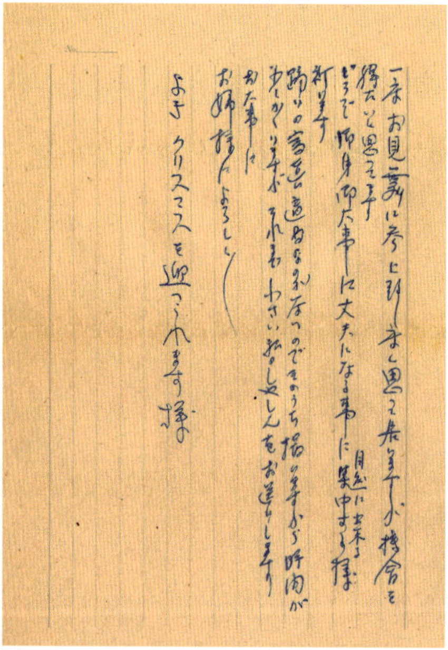

Letters from Kazuo Ohno
A letter to his student, Naoe Yamaguchi

As always, I'm so grateful to hear from you. I am terribly sorry that I wasn't able to talk about anything of interest or to offer flowers the time your elder sister came.

With respect to your impressions of *Downtown Rain*, I felt as though the dance ended up beset by human weakness, whereas I should have trod the ground and danced.

As you kindly mentioned, I ought to more firmly grasp my inner life and render it abstract. How regrettable. I believe that a professor of French literature at Tokyo University mentioned that this piece was difficult, and left after mentioning that it was well made. The distance to the point where it sinks into the depths is too great, and while sinking into the depths is a process in itself, it was a blunder not to have done something about it.

I have received various analyses and criticisms; depending on the viewer some are sharp, but everyone seems to like the piece, and while everyone wrote about the points they liked, I think this, too, is an unusual and interesting point.

I felt as though I was being sucked into an emptiness that arose from a lack of interpretative skills, but after reworking and rethinking my work, I am now equipped with quite a fighting spirit. I'm inspired by having a secret on my side that I've yet to avail of. But still, this seems some distance away. I will pursue the matter calmly and dance as well as I can, so that someday I will surely create a good piece.

Thinking of sowing seeds, last year's *Spring Offering*, conversely, was too abstract and the core idea was vague, so I would like to express something more realistic of my inner life. I can't express it in words, so I still have to condense my thoughts before I

dance, so I am currently wondering how come to grips with this year's recital and am contemplating reworking *Warai* (Laughter) with three variations on the theme. I'm thinking to change it to a French-style scene set on the outskirts (theatre). This year's pieces will thus be more condensed, particularly *Mitsu no Warai* with its variations, making it humorous, devilish, and mad-like. In writing this down, it might strike one as a series of three gloomy Chinese characters, but I would like to handle the piece with a light touch. A devilish laughter that surpasses context; a madcap's laughs that makes one think of positive things.

Besides, we are currently grappling with Baudelaire every evening; everybody brings it along for discussion. There is a French fragrance, a modern expression to the intense fierceness of human pursuits. While we clearly realize that we cannot complete it, we will still work on it as much as possible.

I've been writing only about myself, how is your physical condition? Please take good care of yourself, so that you are calm and happy.

Somehow, I always seem to be living the opposite to that.

I would like to visit you, even if only briefly, for a short time and would like to find the occasion to do so.

I'm praying that you can focus on strengthening your body (naturally)

As for the dance photos, I've nothing appropriate to hand, so we will take them shortly. It will take some time, so in the meantime I will send small photos of me.

Take good care

My best wishes to your sister

Wishing you A Happy Christmas

戦争体験
Wartime Experience

1938年8月召集を受け戦地に向かった。中国西北部の小都市、開封に長く滞在した。ニューギニアで終戦を迎え、復員したのは、1946年だった。

In August 1938, Ohno was conscripted and sent to the Chinese warfront. He was garrisoned some time in Kaifeng, a small city in northwestern China. In 1946, he was finally repatriated from a war camp in New Guinea.

159

160.

160. 1938年頃｜休暇で戻った時の家族写真｜妻 チエ、長男 幸人、次男 慶人
Circa 1938, family photo taken during break from military camp. With Chie holding Yoshito and his eldest son Yukito.

161. 1940年代｜中国河南省で
1940s, Henan, China.

161

162

1926	4月、日本体育会体操学校(現日本体育大学)に入学。 12月、徴兵令により札幌歩兵第25連隊に入隊。一年四ヵ月の兵役につく。
1928	3月、除隊。 4月、体操学校に復学。
1938	7月、次男・慶人誕生。 8月、召集を受け、旭川221連隊に陸軍少尉として配属される。捜真女学校を休職。
1939	4月、小樽港を出港、河南省開封に駐留。
1940	第三十五師団参謀部情報主任の任にあたる。200ボルトの高圧線に触れ全身硬直、大やけどを負う。
1944	3月、青島より船でパラオ島に、軽爆撃機でニューギニアのマノクワリへ至る。マノクワリ、ビアク、ソロンと転戦。芋掘り、サメ捕りなど一万余名の兵士の食糧の調達に従事。
1945	8月、ニューギニア島ソロンにて終戦。マノクワリで一年間捕虜となる。
1946	4月、リバティー船にてソロンを発ち、帰国の途につく。 5月、復員。和歌山県の田辺港に到着。勝浦にて疎開していた家族と再会。捜真女学校に復職。江口・宮舞踊研究所に復帰、物置を改造して住み込み、先生に代わって代替稽古を行う。

1926	April: Kazuo was enrolled in the Japan Athletic College (Nihon Taiku Daigaku). December: He was enlisted in Sapporo's 25th regiment of the infantry corps. His service lasted 16 months.
1928	March: Discharged from military service. April: Readmitted to the Athletic College.
1938	July: His second son Yoshito was born. August: Called up to serve with the Asahikawa 221 Regiment where he was assigned as a 2nd Lieutenant. Took a leave of absence from the Yokohama's Soshin Baptist Girls' School.
1939	April: Sailed out from Otaru and was garrisoned in Kaifang in China's Henan province.
1940	Became Chief-of-Intelligence at the 35th Division's General Staff Office. He suffered severe burns after touching a 200-volt power cable.
1944	March: Set sail from Qungdao to Palau Island, and arrived in New Guinea's Manokwari in a small bomber aircraft. Battles in Manokwari, Biak, and Sorong. He made great efforts to procure food for the 10,000 remaining soldiers by fishing for shark and digging for wild sweet-potato.
1945	August: The war ends in New Guinea's Sorong Island. He spent a year in detention in Manokwari.
1946	April: Repatriated to Japan, sailing on a liberty ship. May: General demobilisation. Reunited with his family. Reinstated as physical education teacher at the Soshin Girls' School. Resumed dance classes with Takaya Eguchi and Misako Miya, lived in their storage-space which he renovated, and worked as a substitute teacher for them.

大野一雄からの手紙

戦線より

北支前田(治)部隊本部　大野中尉

私は2月、一時到官勤務を命ぜられましたが、突然に今までの仕事に帰り、前田部隊の情報主任将校として、勤務することになり、残務整理1ヶ月参謀部にあって、頑張っております。(中略)皆さんから来た手紙を、いつも繰り返しては、学校を思い出して楽しかった生活を、戦友と共に、語り合っております。捜真の桜、捜真の塔、捜真の校庭、お昼の音楽、お昼の体操、私はよく、庭で音楽を聞きながら、踊ったものですね。私の部屋で思い出しては、踊ります。熱、未ださめず。終に閣下の前で踊ったのです。踊ったのであります。
先日はシューマンの謝肉祭(作品9)、コルトーピアノ独奏を聞きましたが、久しぶりの音楽で、感涙、涙がこぼれました。(中略)
3月9日付にて中尉に進級。
お陰様と思っております。

（捜真報国団団報、1940年5月31日）

Letters from Kazuo Ohno

A Letter from the Warfront

Hokushi Maeda Osamu Unit Headquarters, Lieutenant Ohno

In February, I was for a time under orders to supervise administrative duties, and now I'm suddenly back at my usual post as Commissioned Reconnaissance Officer for the Maeda Unit. I'm doing my utmost to catch up on a month's backlog.

I read all of your letters over and over again, and tell my fellow soldiers about the happy times back at the school. The cherry blossoms at Soshin, the Pagoda, the Soshin School, music at lunchtime, and my lunchtime breaks when I would often dance while listening to music. I recall dancing in my room. My passion hasn't yet faded. In the end, I danced in front of His Excellency, yes danced. Yesterday, I listened to Schuman's *Carnaval* (Opus 9) played on piano by Cortot. Not having heard music in such a long time, I was moved to tears.

On March 9th, I was promoted to the rank of Lieutenant.

As always, in appreciation of your kindness.
(Shoshin Hokokudan Danho, 31 May 1940)

死海
The Dead Sea

1983年イスラエルで公演をしたとき、エルサレム、ナザレ、ガリラヤ湖などイエスの足跡をたどった。死海を訪れ、創作のインスピレーションを得た。

When Ohno performed in Israel in 1983, he followed the footsteps of Jesus, from Jerusalem, to Nazareth to the Sea of Galilee Lake. He also visited the Dead Sea where he was deeply inspired.

165

166

165-171. 撮影：ヌリート・マッソン＝セキネ
1983, Visiting Israel. photo: Nourit Masson-Sékiné archives

167

168

169

170

171

172

172. イスラエルの女優 ネッタ・プロツキと｜撮影：ヌリート・マッソン＝セキネ
1983, With the Israeli actress Neta Plotzky. photo: Nourit Masson-Sékiné archives

173.

174.

173. テルアビブにて｜撮影：ヌリート・マッソン＝セキネ
1983, Tel Aviv. photo: Nourit Masson-Sékiné archives

174. キブツにて｜撮影：ヌリート・マッソン＝セキネ
1983, Visiting a kibbutz. photo: Nourit Masson-Sékiné archives

家族
Family

父藤造は函館で北洋漁業を営み、ロシア語を話した。母緑は秋田の裕福な家に生まれ、オルガンを弾き、西洋料理を得意とした。

His father Tozo Ohno ran a fishery business in Hakodate and could speak Russian. His mother Midori was from a wealthy household in Akita; she played the organ and was a good cook who would prepare the family Western dishes.

175. 1933年2月｜中川チエと結婚
February 1933, wedding photo with Chie Nakagawa.

176

177

178

179

176. 父 藤造
　　 His father Tozo Ohno.

177. 母 緑
　　 His mother Midori Ohno.

178. 叔父 池田淑人　画家、チェロ奏者
　　 His uncle the painter and cellist Yoshito Ikeda.

179. 父と母
　　 His parents on the beach.

180. 1960年代｜上星川の自宅前にて
1960s, with his family at home in Kamihoshikawa.

181

182

183

181. 妻と息子
Chie and son.

182. 長男 幸人｜シャンソン歌手
His son Yukito Ohno, the chansonnier onstage.

183. 1988年｜函館弁天町の生家の前にて
1988, in front of his birthplace in Bentencho, Hakodate.

142

184

185

184-185. 1989年｜西武百貨店屋上での公開制作｜次男 慶人が演出を、義娘 悦子が衣装を担当した
1989, with Yoshito and Etsuko Ohno in front of Seibu Department Store. Yoshito directed the piece while Etsuko was in charge of costumes.

143

186.

187.

186. 自宅の台所にて｜自分でもよく料理をした｜撮影：ヌリート・マッソン＝セキネ
In the family kitchen where he regularly cooked.
photo: Nourit Masson-Sékiné

187. 1994年｜アヴィニヨンにて｜妻 チエ、義娘 悦子、孫 美加子、ひ孫 祐輝
Four generations of the Ohnos: Etsuko, Kazuo, Yuki, Chie, Mikako.

188.

189.

188. 1988年｜家族の食卓｜すき焼きは定番メニューだった
1988, Sukiyaki menu for the family mealtime.

189. 1990年｜自宅居間にて｜妹2人と孫、ひ孫たちと
1990, Family visit by his two sisters and their children and grandchildren.

インタビュー6

ヨネヤママコ

先生が「ママコさん、ヴォーグを見てね」っておっしゃるんですね。それで買って読んだけれど、まあ、ピンとこない。まあ、ああいうのを猫に小判というのか、野良猫にヴォーグっていうのか。先生は、やっぱり私に、ちょっと洗練されたエレガンスというものを持ってほしかったんだと思います。

　丘をのぼって、捜真女学院まで丘をのぼるんですけれど、道がとっても楽しくて。今は、こういう年齢で丘をのぼるっていうのは大変だなぁと思うんですけど、あの頃は、とても若い女の子だったから、とてもメルヘンに感じたんですね。そして、捜真女学院の中に入ると教会と女学校がある。で、これもメルヘンで、そこでまた大野先生という、いたく清冽な方が教えていらっしゃる。女学校と先生と、この丘と海と。海を見ながら丘を降りてくるわけですから、なんでこんなに、三拍子も四拍子もメルヘンが揃ってるんだろうと。子供の頃はそう思ってないんですけど、今から考えれば、大変な環境の中であれを教えていただいたんだなぁと思うんですね。

そして、丘を降りる近くになると、先生が「あっ、食べてく?」っておっしゃるんですよ。食べてくって言うと、私も気をきかせればいいのに、結構すって言えばいいのにね。一緒に「はい」なんて言っちゃって、先生のうちへ寄って、先生が鍋を出してきて、おつゆを注いで、そこにあるものを全部入れて、鍋料理ができちゃうんです。先生がつくっちゃうんです。で、そこで食べながら、池宮信夫さんっていう、評論家ですか、踊りの、舞踊の評論。池宮信夫さんがいつもいらっしゃって。そのあと、もう、本当に鍋を囲みながら芸術談義になるわけですけど、大野慶人君も時々現れたり、

お兄さんの幸人さんも現れたり、当時はあの二人、ものすごく美男子で。当時はって言っちゃ失礼なんですけど、ものすごい綺麗でしてね、慶人君が特に。

それで、私は私の故郷に電話して、シイタケを送ってくれって言ってね、シイタケを送って、一箱ばかりお渡しするんですよ。そうすると、大野先生のお母さんが、これがまたいい人でね、本当に、昔のいい人。いい人、本当に、もう。シイタケありがとうって、何回も何回も言うんですよ。それは、私が恐縮して食べてるから、そうじゃないようにしてくれようとしてね、何回もシイタケありがとうね、って言うんですよ。大野先生のお母様の、あのいい方が亡くなるときに、すごく苦しまれたようで、大野先生は、「わたしのお母さん」っていうタイトルで公演をやってらっしゃるんですね。熱で布団中がいっぱいになって、布団がね、もう、こう、熱で水浸しになったっておっしゃって、大野先生がタイトルに書かれていましたけど、現実には親孝行できないから、舞台で盛大な弔いをしようと思われたんでしょうね。

2015.1.14

ヨネヤママコ｜マイムアーティスト。1953年大学在学時に大野一雄に師事。一雄自らに「教えさせてください」と声をかけられた。

INTERVIEW 6

Mamako Yoneyama

I recall one thing that Ohno-sensei told me was to take a look at *Vogue*. So, I went and bought it, but I didn't really get what he meant. It was a case of pearls before swine. What could a feral cat like me learn from *Vogue*? I suppose Sensei was hoping that I might become more refined or elegant.

It was really enjoyable to walk up the hill to the Soshin School. Now, at my age, it is challenging to walk up a hill, but as a young woman it was magical. On entering Soshin there was the church and girls' school. Another magical thing there was to be taught by such a selfless person as Ohno-sensei. What a combination: Soshin school, Ohno-sensei, the hill and the sea. As I walked down the hill, I could look over the sea. How dreamlike it was. Back then I didn't think about it, but I now realize what a wonderful environment it was to learn dance.

I recall how after class Sensei would say: "What about a bite to eat." I didn't have the sense to turn down his offer and accepted it. I ended up saying "yes" and would drop by at Sensei's home. Sensei took out a cooking pot and prepared the broth, adding everything at hand into it. Sensei cooked a meal in the pot on the table and we all ate from it. The dance critic Nobuo Ikemiya was always present. We all engaged in a conversation about art while eating at table. Sometimes his sons Yoshito-san and Yukito-san would show up. Back then they were dashingly handsome, though it's impolite to say "back then." Yoshito-san in particular was astoundingly beautiful.

I asked my folks back home to send me shitake mushrooms and gave the Ohnos a pellet of mushrooms. Ohno-sensei's mother, who was truly wonderful, one of those wonderful people in the old times, kept thanking me for having presented them with the mushrooms. She sensed my uneasiness at table and kept thanking me so as to make me feel more comfortable. She was such a wonderful person; it's a pity that she suffered terribly in her dying days. Ohno-sensei created a dance piece called *My Mother*. He told us how she lay fever-stricken in the futon, with vapour rising. Given he couldn't devote his life to her, Ohno-sensei must have come up with that title so that he could mourn for her on stage.

January 14, 2015

Mamako Yoneyama Mime artist. In 1953, while a university student she studied under Kazuo Ohno. Kazuo Ohno himself one day asked her: "Mamako-san, please let me teach you."

花、草、動物
Flowers, Plants,
and Animals

学校には花壇を作り、自宅の庭には季節の花を
植えた。毎日の草むしりが踊りの大切な稽古だっ
た。映画『O氏の死者の書』では豚小屋で踊った。

Ohno tended the flowerbeds at Soshin
School and planted flowers in his own garden. His daily practice of weeding played a
vital role in his dancing. In the film *Mr O's
Book of the Dead*, he danced in a pigpen.

191.　洋光台養豚場にて映画『O氏の死者の書』を撮影
A pig farm in Yokodai was a shooting location for *Mr O's Book of the Dead*.

192. 1987年｜山形県升玉村にて土方巽野辺送り「蟲びらき」｜撮影：会田健一郎
1987, Commemorative performance for Tatsumi Hijikata at Masutama-mura. photo: Kenichiro Aita

193

194

193. 1980年｜ナンシーの運河にて｜撮影：神山貞次郎
     1980, dancing on the riverbank in Nancy.
     photo: Teijiro Kamiyama

194. 1996年｜釧路近郊の鶴居村にて｜影が鶴になっている
     ｜撮影：石坂秀秋
     1996, Tsurui-mura close to Kushiro. His shadow
     forms a crane. photo: Hideaki Ishizaka

195

196

195. 1980年代 | 自宅の庭
 1980s, in his garden at home.

196. 1981年 | ジュネーブの花時計の前にて
 1981, Geneva Flower Clock.

153

197.

198.

199.

197. 1988年｜岡山県牛窓｜オリーブの丘で公演『死海』赤い帽子でアンコール
1988, Ushimado, Okayama. Performing an encore of *The Dead Sea* in a red hat.

198-199. 1981年｜レマン湖にてスイスロマンドのテレビ番組撮影
1981, shooting with *Télévision Swisse Romande* at Lake Geneva.

枝垂れ桜の影になる
Becoming a shadow under a weeping cherry tree.

大野一雄 1906 - 2010

1906年	10月27日、北海道函館に生まれる
1926年	日本体育会体操学校（現・日本体育大学）入学
1929年	帝国劇場にてスペイン舞踊の舞姫、ラ・アルヘンティーナの来日公演を観る
	体操学校を卒業、私立関東学院の体操教師となる
1930年	キリスト教の洗礼を受ける
1933年	中川チエと結婚。石井漠舞踊研究所に入所、一年間学ぶ
1934年	横浜の捜真女学校に就職
1936年	日本のモダンダンス界の中心的存在、江口・宮舞踊研究所に入所
1938-45年	召集を受け、陸軍少尉、のち大尉として華北、ニューギニアで従軍
	ソロンにて終戦を迎え、マノクワリで一年間捕虜となる
1946年	復員。江口・宮舞踊研究所に復帰
1949年	大野一雄舞踊研究所を開設。大野一雄現代舞踊第一回公演（東京、神田共立講堂）
1955年	第十回国民体育大会神奈川大会の開会式のマスゲームを振り付ける
1959年	大野一雄モダンダンス公演（東京、第一生命ホール）。土方巽が舞台監督を務める
1960年	土方巽DANCE EXPERIENCEの会に出演。ディヴィーヌ役、マルドロール役を務める（東京、第一生命ホール）
1965年	暗黒舞踊派提携公演『バラ色ダンス』で土方巽とただ一度のデュオを踊る（東京、千日谷会堂）
1967年	捜真女学校を定年退職し、嘱託として営繕職に就く
1969年	映画作家長野千秋と舞踏映画『O氏の肖像』製作
1971年	長野千秋と舞踏映画『O氏の曼荼羅 遊行夢華』製作
1973年	長野千秋と舞踏映画『O氏の死者の書』を3年かけて製作
1977年	『ラ・アルヘンチーナ頌』初演。演出は土方巽（東京、第一生命ホール）
1980年	捜真女学校を退職。第14回ナンシー国際演劇祭に招待され、初の海外公演を果たす
	『ラ・アルヘンチーナ頌』『お膳』を巡演
1981年	『わたしのお母さん』初演。演出は土方巽（東京、第一生命ホール）。初のニューヨーク公演
1982年	ヨーロッパを巡演
1983年	イタリア、イスラエルを巡演。死海を訪れる
1985年	『死海　ウインナーワルツと幽霊』初演。土方巽演出、大野慶人共演（東京、有楽町朝日ホール）
1986年	オーストラリア、ブラジル、ヨーロッパなどで公演
1987年	シュツットガルト世界演劇祭にて『睡蓮』初演。大野慶人演出、共演。
1990年	イタリアのクレモナにて『花鳥風月』初演
1991年	北海道石狩川河口特設野外ステージにて『石狩の鼻曲がり』
1993年	横浜赤レンガ倉庫にて『御殿、空を飛ぶ』。第42回神奈川文化賞を受賞
1995年	『天道　地道』初演（慶應義塾大学日吉キャンパス）
	ダニエル・シュミット監督による映画『KAZUO OHNO』に主演
1997年	妻、大野チエ逝去。イタリア、ブラジル公演
1998年	国際演劇協会（ITI）のメッセンジャー・オブ・ザ・イヤーに選ばれる。第47回横浜文化賞受賞
1999年	ミケランジェロ・アントニオーニ芸術賞受賞。ニューヨークにて『20世紀への鎮魂』。最後の海外公演
2001年	東京国際舞台芸術祭で『花』公演（東京、新宿パークタワーホール）。第3回織部賞グランプリ受賞
2002年	第1回朝日舞台芸術賞特別賞受賞。イタリアのボローニャ大学に大野一雄資料室が開設
2003年	函館・金森ホールにて『我が母の教え給いし歌』
2004年	横浜・BankART1929にてKazuo Ohno Festival。以後、毎年開催される
2006年	各国で大野一雄の100歳を祝う催しが開催される
2007年	神奈川県立青少年センターにて百歳を祝うガラ公演『百花繚乱』
2010年	6月1日16時38分永眠

Kazuo Ohno 1906 - 2010

1906	Born on October 27th in Hakodate, Hokkaido
1926	Enrolled in the Japan Athletic College
1929	Saw "La Argentina" Antonia Mercé's performance at Tokyo's Imperial Theater
	Began his teaching career as a physical education instructor at the Kanto Gakuin, a private Christian high school
1930	Baptized as a Christian
1933	Married Chie Nakagawa. Attended the Baku Ishii Dance School for one year
1934	Took up a teaching post at Yokohama's Soshin Baptist Girls' High School
1936	Enrolled in the Takaya Eguchi and Misako Miya Dance Institute, which was to initiate the Japanese modern dance
1938-45	Called up into the military to serve as a 2nd Lieutenant, and later as a captain in Northern China and New Guinea
	The war ended in New Guinea's Soron Island. He spent a year in detention in Manokwari
1946	General demobilization. Resumed dance classes with Eguchi
1949	Established the Kazuo Ohno Dance Studio. The first Kazuo Ohno Modern Dance Recital at Kyoritsu Kodo Hall in Tokyo
1955	Choreographed "Beauty and Strength" for the opening ceremonies of the 10th National Sports Festival in Kanagawa 1959 Kazuo Ohno's fifth modern dance recital at the Daiichi Seimei Hall in Tokyo. Tatsumi Hijikata was a stage director
1960	Danced as Divine and Maldoror in the Tatsumi Hjikata Dance Experience at the Daiichi Seimei Hall in Tokyo
1965	Danced his one and only duo with Tatsumi Hijikata in Ankoku Buyo Performance *A Rose Colored Dance* at the Sennichidani Commemorial Hall in Tokyo
1967	Retired from his teaching position and continued working part-time as the repairman at the Soshin Baptist School
1969	Collaborated with the filmmaker Chiaki Nagano in the making of *Portrait of Mr. O*
1971	Worked on the 2nd of Chiaki Nagano's trilogy, *Mandala of Mr. O*
1973	Started to work on the 3rd of the Trilogy, *Mr. O's Book of the Dead,* which took 3 years to complete
1977	Premiered *Admiring La Argentina* at the Daiichi Seimei Hall in Tokyo, directed by Tatsumi Hijikata
1980	Retired from Soshin Baptist School. Participated in the 14th Nancy International Theater Festival in France, which was to be his first overseas performance. Presented *Admiring La Argentina* and *A Table or a Dream of a Fetus*

1981	Premiered *My Mother* directed by Tatsumi Hijikata at the Daiichi Seimei Hall in Tokyo. The first tour in New York
1982	Toured in Europe
1983	Toured in Italy and Israel, where Kazuo visited the Dead Sea
1985	Premiered *The Dead Sea: Viennese Waltzes and Ghosts* directed by Tatumi Hijikata, and co-performed with his son Yoshito Ohno
1986	Toured in Australia, Brazil and Europe
1987	Premiered *Water Lilies* in the Stuttgart World Theatre Festival, directed and co-performed by Yoshito Ohno
1990	Premiered *Ka-Cho-Fu-Getsu (Flowers-Bird-Wind-Moon)* in Cremona, Italy
1991	Outdoor performance *Hooked Nose Salmon of Ishikari* at the Ishikari River, Hokkaido
1993	*The Palace Soars Through the Sky* at Yokohama Red Brick Warehouse. Awarded the 42nd Cultural Award from Kanagawa Prefecture
1995	*The Road in Heaven, The Road on Earth* at Keio University's Hiyoshi Campus. Starred in *Kazuo Ohno,* a short film directed by Daniel Schmid
1997	His wife, Chie, passed away. Toured in Italy and Brazil
1998	Chosen as a Messenger of the Year by the ITI (International Theater Institute). Received the 47th Yokohama Cultural Award
1999	Awarded the Michelangelo Antonioni Prize. *A Requiem for the 20th Century* in New York, which was to be his final overseas performance
2001	The last solo performance *Flower* at the Shinjuku Park Tower Hall. Awarded the 3rd Oribe Prize
2002	Received a Special Award in the 1st Asahi Performing Arts Awards. The Kazuo Ohno Archives opened at Bologna University, Italy
2003	*The Songs we learnt from our Mother* at the Kanamori Hall in his hometown, Hakodate
2004	The Yearly Kazuo Ohno Festival began at BankART 1929
2006	Many events were held to celebrate his centenary birthday all over the world
2007	*Hyakkaryouran Gala Concert* at the Kanagawa Prefectural Seishonen Center Hall to celebrate his centenary
2010	Passed away on June 1st

この書籍は下記の展覧会のカタログとして製作されました

これはダンスか?「大野一雄」は終わらない。
大野一雄展 日常の糧 〜103歳で逝った舞踏家の生活をたどる
2018年9月28日(金)〜12月8日(土)
会場:若山美術館 Media Art Gallery 5階企画展示室
(東京都中央区銀座2-11-19)
主催:若山美術館
共催:NPO法人ダンスアーカイヴ構想
協力:大野一雄舞踏研究所

Kazuo Ohno Exhibition Daily Bread
Examining the daily life of the Butoh dancer who passed away at 103
Dates : Fri., 28 September – Sat., 8 December, 2018
Venue : Wakayama Art Museum
Presented by Wakayama Art Museum
Co-organized by NPO Dance Archive Network
Acknowledgement : Kazuo Ohno Dance Studio

大野一雄展を開催するにあたって

大野一雄さんを私たちが知ったのは、1929(昭和4)年1月に一雄さんを帝劇に「ラ・アルヘンチーナ」公演に誘った門田義雄さんの息子・秀雄さんが2000年より2年に1回公開していた「彫刻家・入江比呂の家」に来られた大野慶人さんとお会いした時から始まります。今想うと、あの「ラ・アルヘンチーナ」でのおふたりの出会いが、不思議なご縁で今日につながっているのを感じます。ただ、残念なことに私たちが初めて一雄さんにお会いしたのは2010年6月1日のお亡くなりになった日でした。
この展覧会は、私共を含め大野一雄をよく知らない方々にも知って頂くための展示になります。
この国に生まれこの国の世紀にわたる時間を取り込み「舞踏」という作品に仕上げた「大野一雄」という人を今こそ知ってほしいと願います。

On the Occasion of holding the Kazuo Ohno Exhibition

We first got to know about Kazuo Ohno when we met Yoshito Ohno at the sculptor Hiro Irie's house, which Hideo Monden has presented every two years after 2000. Hideo's father, Yoshio Monden invited Kazuo Ohno to see La Argentina perform at the Imperial Theatre in January 1929. When we now look back at that original encounter between Ohno and Yoshio Monden, it feels as though that mysterious link continues until this very day. Unfortunately, however, our first encounter with Kazuo Ohno was on the day of his death on 1 June 2010.
This exhibition is for people who are not familiar with Kazuo Ohno, including ourselves. Through this exhibition, we would like as many people as possible to come into contact with him. We would like for you to now get to know Kazuo Ohno who was born in this country and who crossed generations of this country to ultimately create the artform "Butoh."

展示風景｜撮影：若山美術館写真部
The exhibition at Wakayama Art Museum. Photo: the Museum's photo team

159

これはダンスか？		Is this Dance?
大野一雄は終わらない		"Kazuo Ohno" is still among us.

2019年10月27日初版第一刷発行

First edition on the 27 October 2019

発行	若山美術館	Publisher: Wakayama Art Museum
	104-0061 東京都中央区銀座２－11－19	2-11-19 Ginza, Chuo, Tokyo 104-0061
編集	NPO法人ダンスアーカイヴ構想	Editor: NPO Dance Archive Network
編集協力	呉宮百合香	Assistance with editing: Yurika Kuremiya
デザイン	北風総貴	Design: Nobutaka Kitakaze
翻訳	ジョン・バレット	English Translation: John Barrett
協力	大野一雄舞踏研究所	In conjunction with: the Kazuo Ohno Dance Studio
	捜真女学校	Soshin Girl's School
	上星川幼稚園	Kamihoshikawa Kindergarden
	飯名尚人	naoto iina
販売	有限会社かんた	Sales/Distribution: Canta Co. Ltd
	140-0004	5-11-19 Minamishinagawa,
	東京都品川区南品川5-11-19	Shinagawa, Tokyo 140-0004
	TEL・FAX 03-3450-6507	Phone : 03-3450-6507
	Email info@canta.co.jp	Email info@canta.co.jp
印刷	株式会社シナノ	Printer: Shinano Co. Ltd.

All right reserved ©2019 Canta Co.Ltd   ISBN978-4-902098-10-5

カバー写真：ボブ藤崎   Cover photo : Bob Fujisaki